THE EYES OF THE GOSPEL

THE EYES OF THE GOSPEL

Archbishop Joseph M. Raya

MADONNA HOUSE PUBLICATIONS
COMBERMERE, ONTARIO, CANADA

Second edition 2006 (First published by Dimension Books, Denville N.J. 1978)

Printed in the United States

Library and Archives Canada Cataloguing in Publication

Raya, Joseph M. (Archbishop)
 The eyes of the Gospel / Joseph M. Raya.

ISBN 0-921440-96-0

1. Catholic Church--Byzantine rite, Melchite--Doctrines.
2. Spiritual life--Biblical teaching. I. Title.

BR121.2.R39 2006   230'.19   C2006-902120-1

Cover: Pantocrator (Sinai), 6th century. St. Catherine's Monastery, Mount Sinai

Graphics: Deacon Robert Spencer

CONTENTS

PROLOGUE

A SHARING

To my fellow bishops of the United States of America and of Canada.

To you, my beloved brothers bishops of the United States and of Canada I dedicate this book. I wish to share with you some aspects of the Eastern or Byzantine way of life in Christ. The essence or substance of East and West is the same: there is but one Christian spirituality. Viewpoints and emphases can be different, but the essence is one. Both outlooks are valid, and they should complement one another.

This book will concern itself with the message of Christ in the Gospel: The Eyes of the Gospel. How did Christ see Creation, people and events of life? "Gospel" indeed means one thing and one thing only Good News, a celebration. It means that God is himself a celebration. Consequently, all of creation man, animals, organic and inorganic life each at its own level is also a celebration.

A celebration is a drama woven out of fun, mystery and holiness. It is an ecstasy in admiration. The Eyes of the Gospel are the mirror of this ecstasy, the dynamic process that gives it substance and form. The Gospel brings to life the reality of God and the reality of man. The whole gamut of life from birth to death and on into eternity comes alive in the vibrant voice of Christ as he emphasizes flaming, creative truth, and speaks of the beauty and richness of the daily relationships of God and man.

I am not creating a new form of theology here, only giving it a personal emphasis. I am less clear-sighted than most, less intelligent than many, and not in the least "intellectual." My gift is this: that what happens to another has always had a deep and lasting effect on me. This has been the characteristic of my priesthood for the past forty years. That is why I dare now speak these silent echoes with a loud voice.

The daring is not all mine, not mine only. For I am sad to see so many Christians simply making a list of the wrongs of life the injustices, the horrible deeds, the destructive elements. There is or has been a wave of sadism among Christians who constantly tend to criticize and defame whatever does not come up to their noble expectations and desires. It is time for us to take stock of our dignity, of our inner beauty, and of the high calling God has chosen for us. This book concerns itself with these things. The book sees with the Eyes of the Gospel. If this book contains a criticism, it is that of the artist who, after having admired the tableau of his master, with awe and love takes his brush to add brightness and color to what needed a touch of beauty.

For many years as a priest, and like so many of my fellow priests, I lived in solitude with myself, and in the marketplace with others. Like any other priest, I sat at the banquets of sinners and at the tables of the just and the good. I spent years in the silence of administration, and on the throne of power and glory. I dined with Kings, and slept on the bare ground. I ate sumptuously, and fasted in front of the Knesset of Israel.

Like all my fellow priests and bishops, I am fully aware of the need for a simple, childlike message of hope and joy. Our journey to the resurrection is strewn with failure and success, discouragement and enthusiasm, with trials, tribulations, loves and hates. We are creatures of magnificence and destitution, of heartaches and exaltations. We all recognize the need for continual growth.

Even the divine food of the Body and Blood of Christ does not bring us to the end of our journey. Its reception is rather a push forward to an everlasting beginning, and a beacon of light to guide our steps. We may judge ourselves too severely sometimes; we may judge others, and thus retard or distort our and their spiritual maturity. We can thus create that hell which Christ refused to see in his followers. What a deep sadness in the sound of his warning: "What would it profit a man to gain power over the whole world if he lost his soul." What would man be without his soul!

Many deeply religious psychiatrists readily admit today a type of problem which they cannot solve on their couches. They have healed many types of sicknesses, but there is no cure for those who have "lost their souls," their personalities, and have no virtue; fretting discloses a penchant to enslavement and to a pusillanimous approach to God. Yet, both anxiety and pusillanimity are so common, especially in the

Christian attitude towards life. Looking with the Eyes of the Gospel will awaken the Christian consciousness to its grandeur, beauty, and dignity. The Eyes of the Gospel focus on God, nature, humanity and eternity, seeking to delve into the very essence of being with awe an admiration.

"What is truth?" One has to be a blind Pontius Pilate to believe that truth is something that one can possess, or that there is only one solution to any given problem. On the contrary, the Christian believes that one can only be possessed by the truth, and therefore, solutions to our problems are multiform. The hatchet is the favorite instrument of those who judge others without discussion. Let us remember that the hatchet was at the heart of the pile of arms carried by lectors, the bodyguards of dictators. The healthy attitude of the Christian against the temptation of using the hatchet is sharing. Sharing is the message of the Gospel, the Eyes of the Gospel, the attitude of Christ. It is his Kingdom. Celebration is sharing.

Joyfully I wish to share with you what I am!

Born in the East, I am an Easterner. Born in the land of Sam, I am a real Semite, and not just spiritually! Made from the same clay assumed by the Son of God, I feel, like all Easterners, a certain kinship with the Lord and with his Mother. We are cousins! We deal with a blood relative of the same outlook, mentality and genetic characteristics.

My childhood schooling was with French Sisters. These were of the Roman rite and mentality. But my mother would never allow me to bring home the book called "the Catechism." My good and holy mother used to say, "Catechisms are only good for the Romans. They were written by smart theologians. The Gospel was written by the Lord himself. Liturgical books were written by saints and sinners like us. I want Christ, and his followers the saints and sinners, to teach my children their Christian life. Smart intellectuals belong only in schools."

I thought my mother was really infallible! With her, I read the Gospel and the liturgical books. In my mature years I steeped myself in the Fathers, both those of the desert and those of the "big cities." Actually, I have grown in the manner of a tree. First, I blindly pushed my roots to the very sources. Only today do I dare to spread my branches!

Once I arrived at a certain age I studied scholasticism with gusto and enthusiasm. This was in the seminary of the White Fathers in Jerusalem, near the École Biblique of the famous Lagrange. Augustine and Thomas, Suarez and Bellarmine and Bonaventure were the flags of victory we waved against the Gentiles Marx, Spinoza, Darwin and against all the "isms" which did not bow their heads before the unconquerable syllogism. All heaven was in our heads!

After a long, arduous and most happy apostolate in Birmingham, Alabama, I was elected Archbishop of Akko Haifa Nazareth and all Galilee. I spent six blessed years at the foot of the Master. The atmosphere of the Holy Land (or rather the Land of the Holy) is still vibrating and alive with the "Presence." I inhaled his breath. I saw with my naked eyes the aura of his footsteps. I stumbled on the very rocks he caressed or kicked around. I preciously stored the dust in my breast. (Is not the very same soil that a gardener digs or turns over always responsive, always fertile?)

During these six years in the land of the Lord, my whole scientific approach to God melted away. I experienced my kinship with the Lord. I rediscovered my Oriental and Semitic soul. The Fathers of the desert came alive in my heart. The Fathers of the Church Basil, Chrysostom, the two Gregories these became my daily bread, light and life. Their writings illumined all that a priest of God wishes to have come alive in him. Heaven left my head to dwell in my heart. Spiritual riches, like material abundance, are motives for thanks. But those who are really grateful try to share their riches with others.

The abundance of quotations may be the best part of this book! I do not apologize for them. By using them I only show my admiration and gratitude. This is a kind of humility I am learning at Madonna House. Great, silent "startzy" of old have been born in our midst. Let me mention with emotion the late Reverend Eddie Doherty, the Irishman who became, in his advanced years, a priest of the Eastern rite. I mention also his wife, Baroness Catherine de Hueck Doherty, foundress and ever inspiring leader of Madonna House. My thanks and gratitude to my fellow priests, especially Archimandrite John Callahan my mentor, Rev. Robert Wild my inspiring beacon, and Mary Davis the holy and indefatigable "deaconess."

I would have to be naïve to think that anyone would spend so much time reading such a long preface!

Metropolitan Joseph M. Raya

Former Archbishop of Akko Haifa Nazareth and all Galilee

CHAPTER 1

EXPERIENCE OF LIFE

God is Celebration!

In his Trinity he is Celebration.

In his creation he is a Celebration.

In his dialogue with his creation he is a Celebration.

In the Incarnation of his Son and in the whole work of salvation he is continual and never ending Celebration.

God is not static. His goodness and love are not static either. They are dynamic, infinitely charged energies everflowing in unreserved communication into both his inner life of the Trinity and into creation. In the Trinity we know that God sends the Son and spirates the Holy Pneuma from all eternity to all eternity. Latin Theology calls this inner activity of God "Procession." "He proceeds" from the Father. Greek theology calls this "Perichoreisis" a going around, a dance, a choreography of the divine Person, implying something of a rhythmic and joyful playfulness. God is eternal celebration of love and life.

THE EXPERIENCE OF GOD

God is the great Living One and the Supremely Alive. He made us in his image and likeness alive and forever searching for more life and for the plenitude of life to which God destined us and called us. The radiance of God is indeed life, eternal life, eternal light and a never ending joy. He invites his creation, and especially us, to absorb his abundance of life and light and thus attain to the fullness of joy. He invites us to live the fullness of life and joy and to enter the Feast, to be a celebration. The Feast will become ever brighter and ever more joyous.

When the Feast reaches its zenith, it will become an ecstasy of immeasurable proportion. It becomes celebration: when we experience it we also become a celebration.

If we encounter death, it is not God who created it. It is we ourselves who, by abandoning God, the Living One, create our own death. God is life and cannot be but Life Giving: "I am the Life," he said. "I have come," said the Lord, "so that they may have life and have it to the full." If there is darkness in us, it is not the doing of God. God is Light: "I am the light of the world. He who walks with me will never see darkness." God cannot be the author of darkness. It is we who create darkness and loneliness by rejection light and refusing to follow the Author of light.

Because God is goodness, he cannot force himself upon us. He does not open the door. He rather "stands at the door and knocks." He offers, and he expects us to open to him and freely accept his offer. The gift of God is a grace, an invitation to his own Self revelation which cannot be life giving unless accepted.

It is in an attitude of prayer that we can receive such a revelation. It is in an attitude of listening to the voice and to the invitation of God that we can receive life. God's self revelation is always present. Only by hard work and self imposed discipline, by concentration and self dedication, can we experience the goodness of creation and union with God. Then, and only then, will come the overwhelming knowledge of being forgiven, of being re-created, of being free and of being loved. Being together with others becomes also an overflowing generosity of forgiveness to others, an amazement and an admiration, a joy and a feast. We become a celebration. We cannot induce this authentic transfiguration of ourselves and enter into the Feast, unless we recognize first its spiritual Source and Author.

When we define ourselves by the standards of rationality and power, we become self centered. We imprison ourselves in intellectual categories and absolutes and refuse to abandon ourselves to life and to light. Consequently we lose our capacities for celebration and for the Feast. We become inquisitors, crusaders, persecutors, and we wave the flags of war. We even destroy life and darken creation. There is a definite connection between the celebration of life and the experience of God.

In the past years the world and the Churches of God lived in the security of philosophical formulations. Today, after what humanity has seen of wars how wars bring destruction and inhumanity the Churches of God and the world in general realized that philosophical formulations were false securities. The Second Vatican Council halted the over emphasis on intellectual formulae and reconsidered "Life in Christ." Indeed, faith in Christ is life in Christ. It is not something one possesses. It is being possessed by Someone. Life in Christ is a search and a pilgrimage towards God. It is an adventure in beauty and not a philosophical search. After the Second World War, the cry of humanity became louder and more urgent. It was asking for a positive experience of God and a meaningful answer to the real purpose of life. Humanity wants to be possessed by life. The youth of the world rejected all traditions and roamed the broad roads of life searching for meaning and for God. They were looking for the Feast.

They turned to shouts of triumph and to demonstrations of power and violence. Everywhere, in America, London, Paris and Tokyo, youth sought the ecstasy of the Feast in revolt, in destruction, eroticism and drugs. God and the Feast were not there. Then they turned to communes, to the gyrations of the body, and to every kind of exhibitionism, and to Eastern theosophies and Yoga. What the modern world considered to be the Feast proved rather to be sadness, a taste of ashes and a smell of death.

The celebration of our modern revolutionaries, and the celebration of the Feast of God are, in some way, identical, but they do not follow the same order. For the revolutionaries, exaltation must come first; exaltation is sought for exaltation's sake. But the exaltation ends in disappointment. For them, intensity of life must be first, but it ends in fatigue and despair.

For the Christian, on the contrary, it is rather disappointment that comes first, the disappointment in one's own capabilities and limitations. This disappointment makes us open to God who pours himself into us and becomes our life and our light. For Christians, repentance and death to self and to our insensitivities come first; then, and only then, can we open our eyes and become capable of seeing the flame of things. It is in prayer and self dedication and self discipline that we can experience the presence of God. Indeed, it is only in a humble attitude of prayer, of listening to another, that our hearts can be gripped by a divine atmosphere descending from on high. God makes himself known in an ineffable manner which no philosophy can induce and no human word can express or explain.

The Divine atmosphere overshadows the whole person and

becomes so enveloping that one comes to a point where he wishes to dissolve in it and keep forever its heavenly character. Everything becomes, and all at once, real and beyond reality. Even unreality becomes reality. Something new is added to our perception. Our inner eye opens to a light that brightens and glows. An unknown world comes suddenly into a new focus which we thought never existed and yet which we suspected existed. The Holy Spirit comes to settle down in us in such a way that everything else appears unessential and unnecessary. Life, beauty, light and joy play together, mingle together, and they become an explosion of love and a sharing of paradise. This is the experience of God. This is the Feast. This is celebration.

Celebration shatters logic and all the ordinary securities of sciences and technologies in order to make room for a grace filled presence of serenity. Routine is disrupted. Broken up also is the will for personal power and domination. Self centeredness disappears. We become flames of joy. We experience the immensity of God's design which takes on a new look and seems to be without end. We do not possess this experience. We do not possess the Feast and the celebration. We are possessed by it. Once possessed, our whole being vibrates to the rhythm of the Infinite himself.

One cannot describe it. Rather we burst into praise, admiration and shouts of joy. When Mary encountered her older cousin Elizabeth, and realized all the marvels of the circumstance, she said: "My soul magnifies the Lord…" Martin Luther explains that Mary did not say, "I magnify the Lord…," but "my soul magnifies…," meaning her whole being. All her powers of love and her whole being elevated her beyond herself. In such an experience we realize our frailty. We realize that we cannot by ourselves induce or condition such a beautiful experience. Only God can reveal himself. The exaltation in joy, the Feast, the Celebration creates In the heart a sense of deep humility and dependence on God.

CHAPTER 2

EXPERIENCE OF LOVE

By nature, we are lonely and lonesome for the realities of life. The deeper the realities are, the more eagerly we seek to discover them. Our hunger and thirst for life consume us until our search is satisfied. Verbalization about life does not have much hold on our hearts nor on our imagination. We want to plunge into life's river, live it, and experience its ebbs and flows. Our instinct for life is so powerful that all our acts and thoughts are directed to it. We do not seek only the natural, superficial side of life. We seek a fuller, more complete expansion of all our faculties and the unfolding of our bodily, intellectual and spiritual forces.

To live is to act; it is, indeed, to think and to act the thoughts acquired. To live is, at the same time, to create goodness, wholeness, and increase one's capacity to experience the whole sweep of reality. The instinct for the full experience of life is so powerful in us that we shiver every time we encounter real life. When we recognize, in the depth of our soul, the divine revelation of its intensity, we shiver and thrill, and become inspired artists, poets, saints or lovers. To recognize the reality of God, one has to experience life.

Only a person who has listened to the divine revelation of beauty and love can recognize the fullness of life and experience it. Only when we have experienced it can we not only talk about it but witness to it. Only a prayerful person, a person who is open to listen, can attain to such a level. Because Christ is the perfect, prayerful man, he enjoys the fullness of revelation and can, therefore, open new horizons onto God and onto humanity, and make us discover their wondrous meaning.

Christ knows God, because he is God from God. He has the fullness of divinity. When Christ talks about God, or about life, his very words are life and a witnessing to life. He testifies to his own life. He plays in his own experience, and he moves in it freely, joyously and with ease. He uses poetical words and images to describe God who is all tenderness and fullness of life. To show God in his divine reality as a Father, and as a never ending celebration of life and of love, Christ uses poetry and little stories. Even his silence reaches to the very depths of God where the most eloquent words fail. Besides, Christ is the example of perfect human living because he accepted life unconditionally and lived it fully.

God's reality belongs to the realm of the self evident and self explanatory. God does not have to be proved; he cannot be proved. He is revealed. Those who are open to hear his voice will see him and know him. God is like the sun, the moon, the light, and the air that we breathe. Here they are! And how wonderful it is that they are! God is! How wonderful it is that he is! There is something here that speaks infinitely stronger than any demonstration; it is a loud flourish, a radiant burst of certitude. God is! "The friend of the bridegroom hears his voice and his joy is complete."

There is much more in the statement that "God is." God is a living "Person" and not an idea, or another value. The Universal God of the old religions and philosophies is present now in a bodily form. He is Jesus Christ. This is the awesome mystery of God's reality where truth, the fullness of truth, resides, and whence it flows to infuse every reality and to give it meaning. Jesus Christ is the Being who gives the breath of life and enables every living being to journey to its center. In Jesus, the abstract becomes concrete reality, and God takes on a smiling countenance, a human face glowing with light. No amount of information can reveal him. No amount of intellectualization can reveal a human person as much as one smile or one word coming out of that person's heart. The Christian religion its prayers, its ceremonies, its events and all its teachings are geared to reveal a Person, and to enable us to experience the smile that blossoms from a Person's heart, the heart of God.

Unlike any other religion, the Christian religion is Trinitarian. It does not believe in "God," simply. It believes in God who is Father Son Spirit. God has a face. He is not a general God but a "Person:" he is Father, he is Son, he is Spirit. When we Christians use the expression "God is Three in One," we do not count members one or three, no addition. We point to an ineffable relation between persons. We proclaim a relation of life. We express the idea that God is not a lonely Being abiding in isolation and separation. He is not that "Eternal Bachelor" as some philosophers called him. God is a community, a family "Persons." He is necessarily and essentially an infinitely dynamic Being who communicates himself. In the inner circle of his life he is eternally generating Son, and breathing Spirit. He also manifests himself in creation, Incarnation, Redemption, Resurrection and Ascension. This activity of God in its infinite dynamism, both in himself and in his outward expression, is called by the word love. We say: "God is love."

If God is a mystery, his activity is also a mystery. "God love" is a great mystery. Human love, which is the image of God's love, is also a mystery.

One should not dare approach love, divine or human, except by listening in a humble attitude of prayer. Science or philosophy cannot discover or explain love. Love has to be lived and revealed to be true and real. It is not a slogan that can be passed on. It is the experience and communication of life, the life of a person sung to the other person, a gift and a revelation that enchants the lover, the poet, and the very air. The word "love" denotes the essence of being, the being of God. Love, be it divine or human, is impelling, full of light, of courage, and of encouragement. What a glory for us to be able to share it with God! All the sacraments of the Church are poems of love which sing it and generously offer it to those who are ready to receive its revelation. In these sacraments or "mysteries," we share and in a bodily embrace the life and divinity of God himself. In these "mysteries" we become the poem of God.

If it is true that love cannot be defined, and no one can explain its essence, nevertheless one can describe its elements and analyze its components. Human beings who have lived love and experienced the wonder of its unfolding activity, can sing of it and celebrate its ecstasies.

THE COMPONENT ELEMENTS OF LOVE

Intuition and experience reveal four distinctive elements, or components, in the act, or state of love. All four are necessary and have to be found together to make up its wondrous reality. Each one of these elements is a beginning and "each beginning is an opening to a new beginning" (St. Gregory of Nyssa). Only what we experience and live can we reveal and witness to. Then, we can describe the marvelous process of life and love and unfold the ecstasy that they contain. In order to help our poor human language and understanding of God, we apply this description and this human experience of life and love to God in his Trinity, to God in the Incarnation, Redemption, and Ascension (by this latter I mean the whole of creation returning to its source and center, the Father). The elements of human love which we are about to unfold are found in all these mysteries of God, but at different levels and by way of analogy. These elements are presence, communication, surrender, and identification.

PRESENCE

The first element or condition of love is "presence." Presence is a simple relation to "another," a simple act of awareness of the "other." A person is a mystery which we cannot know through intellectual knowledge. A person can be known only through the revelation of one's self to another who, in turn, through a special attitude of one's being, listens to the revelation of the other and humbly accepts it. In return, the person reveals himself, or herself, and thus becomes present to the other. "A calling of me outside of myself."

Listening and responding are the attitudes of prayer and faith. Faith and prayer are not, therefore, turning to something and possessing it but accepting "someone" who is looking for "another," and wanting to be possessed by the other! "One must have the eyes of faith to recognize the person, not only the divine Person, but any human person made in the image of God" (Lossky).

A person is present to another person when he or she freely reveals himself "as a person," when he or she freely unveils and exposes himself or herself to another person, who becomes thus necessarily motivated by a "person," and in turn, freely opens and reveals himself or herself "as a person." This reciprocal revelation is a pure act of presence, a relation that binds two persons. This is called "presence." This is the first note of an enchanting symphony and the dawn of a bright sunrise.

A friend is present to a friend when he lays himself open to the one whom he really knows and by whom he is really known: "Do come visit with me and revive my strength. Whatever benefit we once gained together you will preserve for me by being present to me; otherwise I fade away little by little, as a shadow, while the day declines. For you are my breath, more than the air, and so far only do I live when I am in your company, either present or, if absent, by your image" (St. Gregory of Nazianzus to St. Basil).

There is but one sadness in life, to be alone. A God of one Person cannot be love. He cannot be joy and life. I believe in God because he makes me a person and because of him I believe in myself. "I am." It is necessary to believe in one's self, to believe that one exists, in order to be able to communicate with another.

Moved by his love for his creation, the Father sends his Son to be present to creation. He sends him to be present to us whom he invites to receive his Son, to be one with him and through him to become his sons and daughters. The Son becomes present in the Incarnation and invites us to open up to God, to reciprocate the presence, and thus to be united with God in a mutual personal relation of presence. The Spirit also is sent to solidify this interpersonal relation by his own "seal," or presence. Thus the three Divine Persons of the Most Holy Trinity dwell in the person who listens to the revelation of God's presence and accepts it; thus do we really dwell in the Holy Trinity.

God made himself present to us in as many physical and psychological ways as possible. Incarnation, Resurrection, Ascension, Word of God who became word of man (Gospels), the Sacraments, and the Indwelling of the Holy Spirit (sanctifying grace) all are presences of God which correspond to all the presences which we can experience. The presence of God in the flesh and in the "stuff" of the universe is the nucleus and crystallization of the love and life of God given to us and to the world. It is the revelation of deep generosity and unlimited goodness of God.

COMMUNICATION

When the first stage of love, which is presence, becomes real and truly reciprocal, love rises to a higher level, to the second stage which is communication. Presence is meaningful and valid only if it represents a person and refers to a person. Properly speaking, "Person" only exists in God. Man tends and longs for his inner realization by communion or participation in the "Person" of the Trinity. When a man or woman reveals himself or herself as a person to another person, they live and act within the very life of God.

It is impossible to enter into a relation with another person without opening and exposing one's own person to the other. This opening to the other is precisely the mystery of the revelation of one's self, the "giving" of one's self. The other "receives" by accepting the revelation, by being enriched with the giving of the other. He is elevated and purified by the riches of the person revealed. He is raised high above his own confines to the light of the image of God in the other. Communication of a person bears the other person who receives him or her back to his own foundation of being, God. He is then satisfied and filled with light.

When the divine Word of God was made flesh and became Man he expressed, revealed, and communicated to man not only the depths of the divinity but also the riches of all creation. "I am the light of the world. He who follows me…will have the light of life" (John 8:12). Accepting the revelation or communication of the other reveals also one's own person to the other. This reciprocal communication is always a divine light, a light that abolishes distance and solitude. It is a triumph over darkness and fear. The beauty that radiates from such a communication is a reminder of the infinite beauty of the Person of God. People who thus reveal and communicate themselves to each other enter into the fullness of the life of the Trinity.

There are no two faces that look at each other and do not give of themselves. There is no possible way to give without receiving. Love gives a person and receives the person. Human beings know each other as persons by what they utter, embrace and enjoy. Through these activities they know each other and without these activities there is no other way to know a person and to enter into communion with a person. I know a man or a woman through the things they say, accept, reject, embrace, and enjoy. These activities are the outward image of the human person.

I know God only by uniting to Jesus the Man, by being assimilated to him, by expressing him in myself. He reveals himself and gives himself to me as a person in the measure I give myself to him as a person. I know a man or a woman insofar as I open myself and unite myself to him or to her. Opening to another is opening to life and to suffering also because by opening I break my self shell: "It is in losing yourself," said the Lord, "that you will find life." Thus we can increase the flame of love by a complete revelation of ourselves. We can also intensify the flame of "Gehenna" by building around us defenses that make us prisoners of ourselves.

Withdrawal estranges us from others and from our own selves. So we can summarize this doctrine by saying: To give a little of one's self costs much; to give much costs a little; to give all costs nothing but exaltation in joy,. By my generous "yes" or acceptance of the other, I can create the infinity of union; my categorical "no" or refusal to be open can reduce my being to infernal separation.

If there is so much evil in the world it is because God has so little possibility to act. We oppose God by not opening up to him and by not accepting him. In his great love, God concedes defeat and goes into hiding. He limits his All Might, veils all signs of power, and retires into his suffering and silent love. God does not "rape." Any compulsion rapes the human conscience. God does not enter where he is not invited and accepted. Herod chased him away from his land when he decided to kill the babies of Bethlehem. God identifies with the innocent and all those who suffer. He cries with them and suffers in them. This is another aspect of the "kenosis" of God. God never forces the evil doer to be good.

Since God is a real Lover, he is never discouraged. He comes back again and again to "knock at the door" (Ap. 3:20). He does not enter unless one opens. The Son of God comes on earth to sit at the "table of sinners." Christ accepted Judas and offered him generously all he offered the others. Judas did not open the door and thus he created hell for himself. On the contrary, the adulteress, the Samaritan woman, the thief on the cross, Zaccheus the abhorred tax-collector-all received the gift of Christ and opened themselves to him in self giving. The encounter with Christ was to them the joy of heaven.

All founders of religions told their disciples to love one another and to love their enemies. The directive to love others, even enemies, is not unique to Jesus. All religions of the earth, not only Eastern religions but the pre Christian religions of the West as well, have a commandment to love the enemy.

The Chinese Li-Ki (Book of Ceremonies) says: "By returning hatred with goodness, human concern is exercised towards one's own person." The wise Lao-Tse emphatically demands "to answer to hurt and injustice with mercy and goodness." Love of enemy has been commandment in India as well as in the Arabian peninsula since times immemorial. We read in the heroic epic Mahabharata: "Even an enemy must be afforded appropriate hospitality when he enters the house; a tree does not withhold its shadow even from those who come to cut it down." There is an old Arab tradition that as long as an enemy or even the killer of one's own family is in the confines of one's own territory, he is to be fed and protected.

The uniqueness of Christ's injunction lies in this: only Christ ever dared to say, "Love as I have loved you." The giving and accepting in love must be generous, complete, without hesitation or condition, and for ever and ever.

The lover accepts the beloved not for what he wants her or him to be but for what he or she is. Christ accepted the sinners as sinners and the sinners became "holy." These sinners accepted Christ for what he was in his reality, and they became divine. Christ is the only One who talks about God as a lover.

And precisely because God is a lover, he is all weakness. If God is a lover he has infinite respect for man, and he is therefore in a position of weakness in regard to his beloved one. He is not responsible for evil. He is rather on the side of the victims, the tortured, the afflicted and despised. It is true that love is strong. It can resist evil and death but it cannot totally succeed unless the loved one is open to love and accepts love. Jesus makes us understand to what extent God is dispossessed in his parable of the Prodigal Son where the Father is thrown out of the heart of his son. He is patient, long suffering; he waits. But when the son returns, the father makes a big feast with no conditions or regrets.

In the Apocalypse, this encounter is called a "supper." To the Oriental mind, "supper" is the supreme time for intimacy and communication of love where one candle lights only two faces. The Christian religion is a religion of invitation, of appeal, and not of obligation or of brutal authority. For this reason it is called a religion of love.

SURRENDER

We have tried to describe love, and we found that the first element in it is "presence." The presence turns into communication of one's self to the other a reciprocal act of "giving receiving." This was the second element or dimension of love. When this "giving receiving," or revelation and communication of one's self is completely accepted by the other, it attains perfection: it becomes surrender. Surrender is the third element of love.

Opening one's self is a liberating movement which must progress until it reaches the frontier of divine reality which is the sublime giving of one's complete personality. The "Giver revealer" becomes the whole life and breath of the other. He or she melts into the other, as the other reciprocates this movement with no less generosity. Each one accepts the value of the other as his or her own. They surrender their own personality, tending and longing for fullness and perfection of union!

Nothing else in this world counts any more. Nothing else has any further value. Each one enters into a new world of play and festivity, of fantasy and ecstasy. Joy breaks through from even a dark background, a joy that can be purified by tears and pain but always overcomes separation and failure in the other. Joy becomes perfect because it knows itself to be joy, and the height of enjoyment is the moment of forgetfulness of self. One closes his eyes to any darkness in life and surrenders himself or herself to uninhibited joy in the face of the other.

Time and space are also completely erased. The lover slows down to God's eternity and one's surrender to the other becomes wealth and joy, saturated with thyme and harmony. This is eternity. The lover is concretely linked and attached to the other who becomes the source and ultimate meaning of being. Such a person reflects the likeness of God. His or her self surrender raises the person, by the surrender of the other, to the heights of the Trinity. Like the joy of the Risen Christ, joy comes to light not in the abstract "love of humanity" in general, but in the individual man or woman, in the personal countenance we see and touch, in "the neighbor's" face. Joy becomes also its own recompense, because in meeting the other we meet and encounter the Trinity. The time of joy is, therefore, the time in which we live now, the time of the present world, the hour of images, and faces, not only the future time of the vision of heaven.

Perfect joy means joy that surrenders, because it stems from the gracious self communication of the "now" of one's self. It bears the stamp of self giving, of spending the self completely without reservation. In the prayer of exaltation and triumph, when the Christian finds himself possessed by Christ in Holy Communion, there is but one cry he utters: "O You who are the fulfillment of the Law and the Prophets, You who fulfilled all the plan of the Father, fill now our hearts with joy and gladness, at all times…" (Byzantine Liturgy). Then a repose in bliss is fulfilled. Inwardly it discloses the surrender of the other which ultimately is the face of the Risen Christ.

Joy is, finally, strong and enthusiastic because its source is always near. It seizes the heart and stirs it with trembling and rapture that overflows in an abundant stream of life. The Holy Spirit overshadows, penetrates, and revives the soul and seals the surrender with his own personal mark which is security and boldness; love becomes persuasive. The lover who thus surrenders finds himself or herself fully in the fullness of Christ and of the Trinity.

Here again, real love cannot admit any condition. The person who opens to the other in complete surrender is received in all his or her totality as they are. Love considers not who is "deserving" or "not deserving," who is "good and worthy," or "bad and unworthy." "God so loved the world that he gave his only Begotten Son." No condition attached. And the Son so loved us that he died for our salvation. No condition here either. God loved us in our "state of sin."

IDENTIFICATION

The fourth and last element or stage of love is identification, in which the lovers become one. Identification is the glorious height of surrender. When surrender touches the very being and attains the awesome degree of intensity, it becomes identification. There is no greater gift than the gift of oneself. A being is fused into another being and melts into it. This is the great mystery of unity in diversity: One and yet so different. In his beautiful sonnet of the "Phoenix and the Turtle" Shakespeare expresses it in this way:

So they loved, as love in twain

had the essence but in one;

two distincts, division none

Number, there in love, was slain.

Single nature's double name

Neither two nor one was called.

Love hath reason, reason none

if what parts can so remain.

When human beings so love one another, or when they experience the bonds of friendship in this intensity, they live the life of the Most Holy Trinity. "God is love, and anyone who lives in love is living with God and God is living in him" (1 John 4:17).

Faith is not submission to or the acceptance of intellectual propositions. Faith is fidelity to a person, faithfulness to a relation, and openness to another, the meeting with God who reveals himself as a person. The isolated individual is not the image of God, but the person in the community of God and men. "Where love is, God is." When I accept the image of God, I accept and receive God himself. "It is not I who live. It is the other." Holiness is nothing else but the constant burning thirst and hunger for the union with the "other." God becomes one with anyone who steps into the orbit of his glory.

I believe that these are the main currents of the Eastern intuitions about love. The hidden dimensions of love are broader than anyone can ever suspect. Only deep silence and ecstatic contemplation can penetrate into them.

In the Incarnation, God is no longer simply God: He is God who became Man. Man after the Incarnation is no longer simply man, but man God. He is divinized, deified. He too has a face and his name is "Child of God." When a woman loves she is not simply woman. She is a love who has a new dimension which arises from her melting into another person. So, man in love is no longer simply a man. He has another dimension arising from possessing and being possessed by another person. The truth of Christ bears all this up and frees it from its own inertia and from our narrowness of thought, for his truth is the truth of love.

The Eastern outlook on God's activity of love and light could be summarized in these four sentences:

There is no God without creation.

There is no creation without Incarnation.

There is no Incarnation without Redemption.

There is no Redemption without Identification with God.

These are the four phases of the one, great mystery of God who is love. And the miracle of miracles consists precisely in this: God giving of himself to identify us with him by deifying us in Christ Jesus.

God's love is not static and unmovable. It is a fact and a never ending celebration in God himself .In us it is a project continually in process of realization. Here the Christian gambles his life on an unending celebration of joy and hopes to make real and meaningful and present what seems remote and impossible. The relation between God and the world, between God and humanity, between God and his people Israel, and finally between God and the cosmos restored in Christ, is expressed in the Bible, the revealed Word of God, in terms of marital union and love.

CHAPTER 3

EXPERIENCE OF THE LOVER

There are no words more ambiguous in our modern language than the word "love" and the word "God." The word "God" is more abused. One wonders about the real meaning behind this word when people utter it in private or in public, jokingly or seriously. Some would declare with bravado that they believe in "God." But a closer scrutiny reveals that their "God" is more capricious Being, now sweet and condescending, now a magical power that a gesture or a word can influence into becoming light or darkness, a smiling face or a vengeful master. This "God" is not the God of the Bible, and certainly not the God of the Gospel.

Other people would declare emphatically that they do "not believe in God." They call themselves and are called "atheists." But when the enlightened religious person sees the idea that lies behind such a "God" which they reject, he too would give their declaration a resounding consent. We do not recognize in what they describe the personal God of the Prophets and of Jesus Christ. In most cases, these so called "atheists" are rejecting a fetish, an idol, a paternalistic father figure, a cruel avenging dictator, a mild, weak monster at the mercy of one's caprices.

The great poet Shelley was a striking example of such a so-called "atheist." Asked by his friend Trelawny why he always bragged about being atheist, Shelley answered: "The word 'atheist' is a word of abuse to stop discussion. It is a painted devil to frighten the foolish and to intimidate the wise and the supposedly good. I use it to express my abhorrence of superstition. I take up the word 'atheist' as a knight took up a gauntlet, in defiance of injustice."

Sometimes also these so called "atheists" are rejecting the notion of

God as an intellectual idea or as a philosophical system. In the Middle Ages, the Roman Church discovered the philosophies and sciences of the pagan world. She "baptized" and "Christianized" its writers, their philosophies and their thoughts. She took their abstract ideas and notions and used them to probe the depths of God. With pagan philosophies at its roots, Christian theology became another "system" of philosophy and another "science." Theologians called it "the Queen science." Theology became a science indeed which created a most impressive intellectual system called "scholasticism." Scholasticism, in turn, created the official language of the Roman Church. Personal inspiration and Christian Jewish origins anchored in the Bible were thus supplanted. The more simple practice of the Church of God in East and West was clearly stated by Tertullian: "Our Christian knowledge and experience of God came to us from the Prophets and from the Gospel of Jesus Christ, not from the philosophers."

"GOD IS DEAD"

Scholasticism and official Roman Church language said everything human intelligence could say about God in precise and perfectly calculated terms. Furthermore, they explained everything that concerned the mysteries of God and of creation in clear categories and left no room for freedom, for new discoveries or new adaptations. There was no room for doubt in such theologizing. Intellectual abstractions and absolutes reigned supreme, with Aristotle and Plato as the living sources of inspiration. Theology became a palace, unassailable and unapproachable, where God was entrenched and secure, separated from the stream of life. Celebrations and liturgies were stifled and became colorless and dead. Once the feast was killed, the world thought that God was also dead"

"Did you not hear," wrote Nietzsche, the prophet of the "God is dead" era, "of that young fool who, in the bursting fullness of one morning's bright light, lit a lamp, hurried to the marketplace and started shouting: 'I am looking for God! I am looking for God! Where did God go?' And he proceeded to say: 'I am going to tell you where God went: we have killed him, you and I. Oh! How did we happen to empty the Oceans? Who furnished us with the sponge with which we wiped out the entire horizon? What did we do to disengage earth from its orbit around the Sun? Do we not feel emptiness blow in our faces? Is not the night coming back on us thicker and more terrifying again and again? Don't we hear anything? Listen to the trembling footsteps of grave diggers. They are no burying God! Don't we smell already some of the divine putrification and stench? God is dead! God is dead!'"

A century after Nietzsche's prophecy, William Hamilton and Thomas Altizer in America and, after them, a score of theologians and philosophers the world over, produced certificates of the death of God. For the past century and a half, grave diggers have been busy singing dirges over the "Death of God," not realizing that Christian intuition and the Gospel of Christ can revive again and cover the nakedness of human philosophies.

The Gospel of Jesus Christ is not static. The Gospel always inspires the search for meaning and ultimately for the transformation of this world into a place where God can talk and move and live and make man come alive. Christians, therefore, cannot stand still. We live in the breath of the Holy Spirit who is an irresistible wind. The real home of our Christian God is no the Greek temple, but rather the Gothic Cathedral, pointing freely to the high heavens and exposed to all the winds and storms, to the twinkling of the stars and to the burning sun. Our home is the Byzantine Church, "Dome of the heavens," that gathers the whole universe into its embrace. God is life.

Christian intuition and the teaching of the Gospel proclaim that God is an experience and not a science or a philosophy. He is a risk, a constant revelation, a mystery, a real mystery of thrill and joy, and not an intellectual security. God is a Lover. Perhaps no human activity has been fraught with more possibilities for the impossible, for ecstasy, challenge, freedom and joy than this Judeo Christian conception of God. With celebration of God's reality as a Lover, the Christian will re create a new cultures that will always enlighten and guide and give hope and salvation. Without this celebration, Christian life and hope and faith will have no impact and probably no meaning.

THE LIVING GOD

The God of the Gospel, the God preached by Jesus Christ, has a face, a clear, well delineated face, illumined and illuminating. This God is not a magician, nor a threatening power, nor a distressing shadow that a trick, a word, or a ritual can at random shackle or release. He is not "opium" either. He is strong, and speaks clearly: "Why are you frightened? It is I" (Mark 4:40). Again and again he shows his face in a bright daylight: "Courage! It is I! Do not be afraid!" (Mark 6:51). Our God has a face. And that face is Jesus Christ who is also the smile of that face. If we can utter a true word about God, it is because one day a man in Galilee spoke. Jesus revealed God not in human terms but in his very person, in poetical analogies and biblical realities. Jesus is the artist of God who through appearances goes into the heart of things, into the heart of people, because he is the heart of God.

The God of Jesus Christ is never presented as an object of knowledge. He is rather an object of union and encounter. We have already explained that a "person" cannot be an object of knowledge. Only love brings discovery of a person. An open face reveals. A mask hides. God is an open face that was revealed by the prophets in hope, and by Jesus Christ in his Person, in his open face. The God of the Bible, and more specifically the God of Jesus Christ, identified himself as the "lover of man," the "Lover of his people." As the "Lover of his children," he is never discouraged, never despairs, is never repulsed by the unfaithfulness or miseries of his beloved one.

The face of God that we encounter in the Bible is astonishingly similar to the face of a human lover. Jesus Christ preached and taught a way of communion and an encounter with the supremely Loving God. Jesus tells us that this God is a Lover, a real Lover, and he describes him with human expressions so that we may be sure of what God really is: a Lover.

Hosea the Prophet had married a wife whom he loved strongly and tenderly. But the beloved woman scattered herself into the winds of unfaithfulness. She prostituted her love. Her faithful husband pursued her, brought her back, purified her, and rebuilt her throne higher and more glorious than ever before. Like Hosea's wife, we whom God has "wedded and loved" can sell ourselves into shame and misery; we can become faithless harlots. But God will always pursue us to cover our nakedness and purify us and restore us to the joy and bliss of his embrace. God is a Lover, and he himself does not hesitate to proclaim it:

I will betroth you to myself forever…

I will betroth you with tenderness and love.

I will betroth you to myself with faithfulness

(Hosea)

It is in this same strength of tenderness that Jesus portrays the Father, our God who "sends his sun and his rain to the just and to the sinner alike…" He invites to his table those who are friends and those who are scattered, the hideaways. He gives to the one who came at the last hour of the day's work as much as to the one who carried the burdens and the toils of a lifetime.

The prophet Isaiah picks up Hosea's story of his relation with his unfaithful wife, how he restored her to his love and intimacy, and applies it once more to he relation of God with his people:

Do not be afraid…for now your Creator will be your husband, his name is God, and your redeemer will be the Holy One of Israel and he is called the God of the whole earth. Yes, like a forsaken wife, God calls you back. With great love I will take you back (Isaiah 54,4-6).

God does not tire of revealing himself as a Lover who is never driven away by the unfaithful escapades of his beloved one: "I shall wed you forever…I have loved you with an everlasting love" (Jer. 31,1).

The most glorious revelation of God as a Lover bursts out in a powerful festive poem called the Canticle of Canticles, the last verses of which summarize the tone of the drama that went on between two lovers, man and woman, God and man. All good Jews and the Lord himself read this poem every week to greet the coming of the Sabbath, the day when the Lover encounters his beloved one:

Set me like a seal on your heart,

like a seal on your arm.

For love is strong as death…

The flash of it is a flash of fire,

A flame of God himself (Cant.).

THE GOD LOVER

There is only one love, God, and God is an ever active Lover. All our human loves are only a dim participation in this resplendent Lover. He is the source of all loves and he himself sets them aflame. Jesus Christ crowns them with honor and glory in every page of his Gospel. Where the Canticle sings of bodily charm and of radiant beauty, of smells and sounds of love, Jesus elevates to a divine level. And he transforms all passing desires into a thirst and a longing which only God can satisfy.

Christ was fully alive to the reality of his Father's love. He sang and displayed the full range of his tenderness and he carried this theme into every story and every gesture of his life. Incessantly he recalls, without using the earthy buoyancy of the prophets' style, the wedding, with all its excitement and delights. For him, the experience of God is a "wedding," or a "wedding banquet," where just and sinners, free men and slaves, rich and poor, weaklings and strong mingle together without distinction or qualification. They are the beloved ones, and God is their Father, their Lover and their Savior. He is a "Bridegroom": " 'Why is it that John's disciples and the disciples of the Pharisees fast, and your disciples do not?' Jesus replied: 'Surely the Bridegroom is still with them? As long as they have the Bridegroom with them, they could not think of fasting.'" How plain and unmistakable the Lord is. Where he is, neither Torah nor law can stop or shorten the joy and bliss of the wedding.

Christ goes so far as to portray himself as a romantic Lover who surprises his "bride" at the most unlikely hour of the night, when "everybody had grown drowsy" and "fell asleep," said the Gospels. "At midnight there was a cry: the Bridegroom is here! Go out and meet him!" (Matt. 25:6). The darkness of the night turns into a festivity of "lights" and "lamps" and glows with foolish and wise girls.

The Christian Church picks up the theme of this Bridegroom and never tires of repeating it in all its beauty: Behold! The Bridegroom is coming!

Behold, the Bridegroom is coming in the middle of the night: blessed is the servant He shall find awake. But the one He shall find neglectful will not be worthy of Him. Beware, therefore, O my soul! Do not fall into a deep slumber, lest you be delivered to death and the door of the Kingdom be closed on you. Watch instead, and cry out: "Holy, Holy, Holy are You, O God!…"

Nowhere in the message of Christ does the inner divine feeling of love come through as clearly and forcefully as in Jesus' farewell speech of the Last Supper. He compares his sadness of leaving his beloved "little children" to the agony of the woman who is immersed in suffering while giving birth. His wish and his heart's desire is for those he loves to be where he himself is, and to possess by grace what belongs to him by right: "Father, I want them to be with me where I am…and so I may be with them" (John 17).

The supreme test of love is to accept "death for the one who is loved." Christ accepted suffering and death for the life of all the children of God, for every person. If there is one thing that is certain in the history of religions it is that the death of Christ put an end to all blood sacrifices. It destroyed all material and human sacrifices. All sacrifices find their completion and goal in Christ's death for humanity. "By one offering he has perfected forever them whoa re sanctified" (Heb.). What really changes hearts is not so much to love as to be loved. The greatest treasure in this world is the knowledge that there is another who will simply stand alongside and share one's inner agony and not be afraid of it. What makes us open to life, to hope, and to joy is when we realize that someone has opened up to us in love. And when we realize that we are loved by a person such as God, we enter into the fullness of life, into the fullness of hope, and the fullness of joy. When we find ourselves living this wondrous realization, our windows onto life come unstuck and open onto paradise. The Holy Spirit explodes in us, makes us sing for happiness and freedom. To be loved is a celebration. Therefore, there is no room any more for anguish, no room for guilt, no regret for any past failure. All our energies and faculties strain forward to that "rest where the sound of rejoicing never ceases, where the delight of those who look upon the beauty of his face has no bounds."

Christians are conscious that if we are saved and divinized it is precisely because we have an intrinsic divine value. We are loved. We have hope because of God's love. We are the children of the Kingdom "not because we have done anything good on earth but because God loved us first." On Holy Thursday the Church does not hesitate in her prayers to use strong comparisons, sometimes offensive to "delicate ears," to make us understand the powerful reality of the love that God bears for us. "What is our holiness, O Lord? What is our goodness, or our good works in your eyes? They are like a repulsive rag a young maiden throws away! Your love is immeasurable and your mercy is without limit."

Christian spirituality, and especially Byzantine spirituality, constantly brings to mind the abyss of sin in which we are engulfed in order to stress much more "the infinite love of the Infinite God" (Gregory of Nyssa). The two contenders, man and God, are always present in the same arena, in our consciousness and prayer: God who loves and man who is loved; God who forgives, and man who is forgiven; God who saves and man who is saved. By himself, a man is immersed in evil and despair, while in God he can always enjoy hope and salvation. "Where shall we hide, O Lord, for our many sins? Shall we run to the mountain top? You are there in your majesty! Shall we go into the abyss of the oceans? There your hand is all powerful! Shall we sink into the depths of the earth? Your breath makes the earth quake! Open your hand, O Lord, open your hand and we shall hide in the palm of your hand...You are the Lover of man."

To the modern atheistic formula, "If God exists, man is not free," The Christian answers, "if man exists, God is not free." Man can say "no" to God. God can never say "no" to man. That I am free means that God exists. In creating us, in becoming our Lover, God made himself vulnerable to the point of accepting crucifixion and death to make us divine. The All Might, and All Power becomes All Weakness. Thus Love is indeed weakness. It is all patient and long suffering.

Once upon a time there was a great King, all powerful and strong. He commanded innumerable armies, and the earth trembled under his feet. He fell in love with a humble peasant girl. He offered her his Kingdom, his riches, his power and all he had. His life was all in her possession. He offered her prayers and entreaties. But as she was all beauty and capricious, she would never answer. The powerful and mighty King could not give her orders to reciprocate his love. He could not force hr to accept his offer. Power and might cannot win a heart.

Pursued by Herod, God does not strike back. He takes refuge in exile. He hides in Egypt and he comes back only when madness has been eradicated. The unfathomable expression of the love of God is found in his respect for human liberty. God created man free, and He limits Himself within that freedom. When God bowed down in all humility before the cruel freedom of man, he made possible the paradox of the cross. As a real Lover, he accepts to be rejected, evicted and expelled. God can do anything and everything except force himself on his human creatures. Refused, he "waits at the door and knocks." He never opens the door.

God cannot therefore stop the evil that we create. Evil and the revolt against evil are proofs of the existence of God and of the infinite love of that Innocent whose face is covered with spit and dripping with innocent blood. One drop of blood of the divine human face of Christ is sufficient to change the universe. But God wanted us to sprinkle that blood freely use it to transform humanity and the universe.

Salvation comes near or stands afar off according to our attitude towards the invitation of God. God is always ready. But he will never force himself into our hearts. God does not "rape."

Abandoned to ourselves, we are agitated by self centeredness, selfishness and fears. We are tossed in all directions by the winds of our solitude and loneliness. We seek refuge upon shores of empty dreams and self images of security. By ourselves, we only encounter absurdities and desolation. We know that we are miserable. But the Christian knows that there is a more miserable One than himself: the Lover who waits. For all he has done for us, God only desires our answer. When we listen to his voice, he acquits us from all spiritual debts and sets us free from our miseries.

St. James writes: "The demons believe and tremble!" They tremble because they do not want to hear the Lover's voice. We also can believe and tremble .We can hide in the vacuum of our hearts and close our ears to the voice that wishes to set free and save. Moderns find the idea of God "sad and depressing" because they conceive him as almighty and yet unable to stop evil and strike back. Such a God is indeed sad!

Our God is rather a presence and a radiance of love. He never shouts. He never strikes. He talks in a whisper. St. Isaac proclaims that "the only sin, the real sin is when man does not listen to his voice and when he is insensitive to the Resurrected" (Sent. 118). God offers and invites. He never gives orders: "Shema, listen, O Israel," "If you want to be perfect…if you want to follow me…if you want to be healed…He who has ears to hear let him hear…" These are this words. Such is God's respect for our freedom.

Our destiny is freedom, joy, fullness of life and fullness of happiness. This is not our invention or a dream. It is the reality of God who offers himself as a gift, a free gift, a generous donation. God is a real Lover. We cannot deserve him. Only "the infinite love of that infinite God" can offer such a gift. He does it freely and unhesitatingly to anyone who heeds the invitation.

For Christians, the measure of their holiness is not good works alone. It is much more the measure of the acceptance of the love of God and of the answer to his invitation. The more we listen to this invitation, the more we become like God. When we become like God, when we abandon ourselves entirely to God, God accomplishes in us all the miracles of his love. He is the One who acts, who moves and inspires. In him, we become strong and powerful. "I can do all things in him who strengthens me." God died on a cross so that we might live in the Resurrection. Real life is the encounter of the Lover. This encounter is realized in Christ.

CHAPTER 4

DIALOGUE OF THE LOVER

THE REALITY OF GOD THE FATHER

Christianity affirms that "God created." Consequently, it affirms also that he is an artist. When that artist, God, looked at his creation, he was pleased. "Well done," he said. It was "very good," says the Bible. And God blessed the world, blessed the man, and the woman, blessed the beasts, and all his creation. He blessed also the "seventh day," time and space. "He blessed them" is an expression in the Bible which means that he filled everything that exists with love and goodness and beauty from his own love, goodness and beauty. God rested from his work, but his love keeps on enlightening, strengthening and elevating us "from glory to glory" to the heights of God's own personal Trinitarian life. He inspired man, he revealed himself to man, and kept calling him in a marvelous dialogue of love which constitutes salvation history and which we call by another word, "tradition." God is a Lover: He dialogues.

In its strictest sense, salvation history means the dialogue that God initiated with his creation from the beginning of time. It is the story of his inner life manifested in his care for creation. God solemnly began this dialogue at the creation of the world. He revealed it personally, first to Noah, then to Abraham, and then to a special people, Israel; he clarified and brought it to perfection in his Son, Jesus Christ. He will maintain it forever in the Holy Spirit who will remain active with creation "until the consummation of the world." This story is also called Tradition, in which God's Word inspires, directs and shapes individuals and nations to the fulfillment of their divine destiny and to the realization of their own history of salvation.

Tradition is, therefore, the revelation of the life of God ever fresh, and always burning with a flame of its own in peoples' hearts and minds. The Word of the Lord is light, and this light will always blaze forth to enlighten humanity. It is not a question of a mere teaching handed down by a uniform repetition. It is rather a manifestation of what God is in himself, and of the pattern of action we should take in our relation with God and with each other. It is far from being a scientific exposition of the world, or a history of the development of mankind's thoughts or philosophies. Tradition is God's movement in the history of mankind, God's Word and God's life revealed. This movement is constantly revealed in the cultures, customs and habits of mankind. All cultures, customs and habits of nations are a revelation of God's love and of God's Providence.

God also intervened in the history of mankind in a very special way. He revealed himself as "Persons," as a trinity of Persons, as Father Son Holy Spirit. This special revelation carried with it the message of God's relation with us as a Father and as a Lover. The greatest fact of human history is the fact that God became man. He became the fullness of revelation. Man saw him, touched him, heard him, and now he can say, "I know God because I know God made man, Jesus Christ."

The highlights of the first movement of the revelation of God were received and kept by a select people who were chosen to be a blessing and a hope for mankind. The people of Israel were indeed set apart by God to receive faithfully, keep, and transmit in all its integrity, the will and the Word of God. These three facts that the revelation of God comes directly from God himself; that it is faithfully received; that it is kept and transmitted in all its integrity comprise the three essential characteristics of Holy Tradition. Israel was chosen by God to be listener, bearer, and keeper of God's special revelation and God's word. In Israel and through Israel, God spoke to the world and showed that he was constantly present in humanity and caring for creation. He entrusted this people with the history of his love and inspired them to record it and to retell it to mankind.

The books which recorded these deeds and words of God before the coming of Christ are called the "Old Testament." The books that recorded the deeds and words of God in his Son, Jesus Christ, are called the "New Testament." Both Testaments put together are called the "Holy Bible." The word "Bible" means book. The word "holy" means "special," "separate," "unique," "awesome." This book is called "holy" because it contains the message of a "Persons" God who is supremely unique, supremely special, and supremely awesome. It is the story of God's love and of God's saving action throughout the history of mankind. It one sentence, it is the life and Word of God: "For the word of God is alive," and life giving, says St. Paul (Heb. 4:12). The Holy Bible is the special book for those who are seekers of God. It is the banquet where we are invited to live and enjoy the impossible.

Naturally, the writers of the Old Testament, being Jews, expressed the divine Word and inspiration of God in terms of Jewish culture, Jewish expressions and figures. To really understand and taste the beauty of revelation of the Old Testament, one has to know and understand the old Jewish history, mentality and culture which are so vastly different from our own. The Prophets of Israel, for instance, recount their experience of God in the events of their daily lives. These experiences should be studied and understood first in their historical setting. Their spiritual message will have resonance only in hearts which are attentive to the voice of God and open to the God who speaks and reveals their meaning.

The Jewish people lived human situations that were marked by extremes, by a mixture of all the tragic realities of life: triumph and glory, exile and silence, return and hope, death and rebirth. The cruelties of wars, the killing of the innocent, "dashing the children's heads on the rock," are all part of the tragic reality of the history of the Jewish people. Such cruelties of man to man are the events of history which God does not condone, much less order, but still, every revelation of God springs from a specific historical, human situation of glory, or moral courage, or weakness, or even wickedness.

Besides the historical facts, and along with them, there is also the cultural situation. The living Spirit of God is like the wind, the air, the heaven, hovering bodiless over the earth seeking a body. He, no doubt, always weaves for himself a body by assimilating what he previously had inspired and what he encounters now in the world as a specific culture.

In the Old Testament the Spirit encountered Jewish culture, and adopted from it the superb use of the five senses with their vibrant expressions. In the New Testament he found the Greek and Roman cultures. To this Jewish cultural base he added the Roman genius for creating order through toil, experience, and speculation. From the Greeks he adopted depth and delicacy of feelings and loftiness of thought, and their respect for the dignity of the human person. The Holy Spirit of

God always takes the cultural forms which he has previously inspired and breathes into them new life. He always inspires and directs humanity in its ascent to God within its present historical situation and mental development. He gives direction to cultures, mentalities and ways of life, and chooses always the best of their elements to weave for himself a body. The Holy Spirit is always recreating the world.

THE REALITY OF THE HOLY SPIRIT

Thus, Tradition is alive with the presence of the Holy Spirit of God, and is therefore composed of two elements. One element is the past, and the other is the present, from which later springs a new creative inspiration. Both these elements existed in the Prophets of the Old Testament. They existed in Jesus Christ, and in the Apostles; they still exist in the Church today and will exist "until the consummation of the world." Tradition, therefore, relies, on the one hand, on the past, and on the other hand, it shakes off the dust of the past that weighs us down and leaps into a new future.

Every prophet had these two elements, fidelity to the past and a breaking with it. Christ, for instance, gathered in a brief synthesis the scattered pieces of old truths, laws, and prescriptions, and then projected himself and all of humanity into a new life of freedom and joy. A Chinese proverb says, "When someone points to a star, the fool looks at the finger only!" The Christian bypasses the finger that points to human frailties, weakness or wickedness, and sees the immensity of the sky, the infinite and unending twinkling of the light of God directing humanity to the Parousia.

The ever active presence and inspiration of the Holy Spirit constitutes the continuity of Tradition. Thus the spiritual reality of the Old Testament is found in the New. Christ makes real and true what was foretold of him as the ground of realization of the figures and promises concerning him. Their truth is this: that they are fulfilled in him. He, then, is the truth of these past events. In his conversation with the two disciples going to Emmaus, the Risen Lord undertook to show that he is the personal focal sense of "all the Scriptures." Thereupon their "hearts burned," and the heart of fire led to the opening of the eyes. The Apostolic and Post-Apostolic traditions, and our liturgical books of today, are continually reproducing the Old Testament figures, stories and even expressions, and applying them to Christ. Indeed, the liturgical service books, and especially in Byzantine spirituality as a whole, are, in the last analysis, little else than one vast and extended meditation upon Holy Scripture.

The sacramentary expositions, as well as the paintings of the catacombs, treat the same historical themes of the Old Testament Adam in Paradise, Noah in the Ark, Moses crossing over the Red Sea. These were all types of Christ. He is the New Paradise. He is the Ark of grace and love that saves the world from drowning and from annihilation. In Christ is the real Passover from slavery to freedom, from darkness to light, from death to life. St. Paul says that "these things (of the Old Testament) come in figures and have been written for our instruction…" (1Cor. 10:11). Even the very gestures of Christ are seen and interpreted in the light of what happened in the Old Testament, which in turn explains them. For the Christian religion, the marvelous deeds of God in the Old Testament and the life of Christ in the New are continued and revitalized in the sacraments and in the life of the Church.

Christianity is one essential revelation, the revelation of Jesus Christ who is the Image of God the Father and the only one who can reveal him and make him known. In Christ, "all the fullness of the Godhead dwells bodily" (Col. 2:9). "The Father transmitted everything to the Son" (Matt. 11:27), and the Son transmitted it in turn to his Apostles. The Apostles transmitted it in the same way to their successors. In order to continue this revelation of God, Christ promised to send the Holy Spirit of God and in face he did send him to abide with his Apostles and their successors "to the end of time."

The Old and New Testaments are of equal honor and value, being together the one record of the one life of the same God. They are also an essential element for the normative articulation of the religious experience man has with God. The community which receives faithfully, keeps and transmits in its integrity what it has received from God the Father, Son, and Holy Spirit, is unmistakably witnessing the presence of the One and unique God who is inspiring and directing mankind to its fulfillment.

The assembly of Christians that gathers in the name of God, to proclaim his work and his life as related in the Holy Bible, is one with the Jewish community, one with the Apostles, and with all those who recognize and honor the word of God. The Christian community identifies with them. The assembly that reads the word of God is the human race in miniature. In fact, such an assembly represents the whole human race. When it reads the Word of God and recalls his deeds of the past, it proclaims also his present action and care.

Furthermore, in order to witness to its identity with Christ and His Apostles, the assembly of Christians always refers to the Word of God, and to the action and movement of God as expressed in the Holy Bible. Our Blessed Lord gave us his divine example by quoting it. The Apostles consistently referred to it. And it was for generations of Christians the sole object of meditation, the center of spiritual life, and the source of theological knowledge. It is not the personal theological expression of the Fathers that draws our attention. The great value of their works consists in reproducing the Apostolic era of which they are witnesses.

The Church constantly refers to Tradition and to the Holy Bible. The Bible and Tradition are called the "Faith of the Fathers," and "Apostolic Tradition." This is the reason why all the dogmatic definitions of the Seven Ecumenical Councils were introduced by such expressions as: "Following the teaching of the Fathers…" The Fifth Ecumenical Council of Constantinople (553) declares: "We confess, hold, and preach the faith which in the beginning our Great God and Savior Jesus Christ gave to his Apostles and was proclaimed by them to the whole world. This is the Faith which the Holy Fathers confessed, expounded and handed on to the Church, and we follow them in everything."

RELEVANCE OF THE DIALOGUE OF GOD

All the above mentioned facts are reasons why we pray from the Bible, why we preach from it, and why we worship and adore in the context which it provides. It is the basis of our Christian liturgy and the source of inspiration for Christian piety. There is hardly a prayer said in the assembly of the faithful which does not reflect a thought or a prayer taken from the inspired word of God. Every Sacrament and liturgical service is woven by quotations from the Bible and includes some reading from it, so that Christians may live more fully the mystery of God in all its awesome glory.

For the first centuries of Christianity, philosophical discipline and reasoned logic were only used as tools in the expression of the mysteries of God. When it was necessary to face philosophical objections and intellectual difficulties, Christians used these tools sparingly and with great repugnance, because there are no theological formulations in the

Bible. According to the Church of Christ, and especially to Eastern Christianity, theological formulae must be verified by biblical tradition.

Tradition is not a blind attachment to ancient times and customs, but a living and dynamic relation with the totality of the experience, life and teaching of God, of Christ and of the Apostles of Christ understood in the light of the Bible. Christian intuition was hesitant in relying upon logic and reason in the sphere of theology. In the first centuries the reliance on logic and reason was even considered as breaking with the Tradition and with the Holy Bible, and it was criticized as such. We cannot restrict the life of the Holy Spirit to a formula, or identify it with a human word or gesture. St. Thomas himself reminds us that, "The word that expresses faith is not what is being said but it points to a reality." The reality of life in God can never be fettered by the sound of words or by intellectual elaborations. The reality of God is a gigantic flow of life that surpasses all intellectual limits.

In the third century, for instance, the Church of Alexandria established the Didaskalion, or school for catechumens, and initiated the beginning not only of doctrinal elaborations, but of a speculative spirituality. The Church repudiated this Alexandrian school of Origen as too exclusively Greek, too rational, too philosophical, and insufficiently scriptural. The didaskalion was short lived.

In the thirteenth century, intellectualism, and later rationalism, invaded the West and penetrated into the Church. Roman theologians thought it necessary to express revealed truths and the nature of our relation with God within a system of human knowledge. They had to find precise and exact terminology in order to remedy Eastern and biblical expressions which in fact provided occasions for misinterpretations. They felt also that since essential doctrines were directly revealed in the Bible, all other doctrines and corollaries could be derived by a kind of Aristotelian deductive process. Once this beneficial, yet dangerous step of rationalization was taken, theology in the Roman Church became predominantly a discipline of the mind and a school for mental exercises, the "queen science," but nevertheless a science.

Reason and intellect were enriched by abstract concepts. Religious thought gained precise notions and exact formulations. But spirituality suffered. Consequently, the "mystic" character of God's love and the incarnational atmosphere of "sacramentality" were lost in the maze of logic. Holy Scripture was neglected respectfully and consciously relegated to a subordinate position. The reading of the Bible in Western spiritual life became almost non-existent, or forbidden for a long time. The road was wide open to modern Rationalism and the dialectic materialism of Marx and Engels.

During this time the Eastern Church was accused of living in the past because of its insistence on Tradition. The Eastern Church, on the contrary, believes that it is rather the past that lives in it, because the past is a reality which happened in their midst, and they are faithful to it. Easterners possess a sense of being in their own forefathers. They feel that the very blood which stirred in the people of Israel and in the human body of Christ still flows in their own veins. The fact that Christ lived as one of their ancestors forms a chapter of their life the single most vivid chapter, it is true but still just one chapter. The Holy Mother of God, the Apostles and those who knew them, the whole collection of oral sayings and stories handed on from father to son legends, tales, lore this is a stream of life whose ebb and flow ties the past to the present. It is with kin, not thoughts, that Christians, and especially Easterners, are linked.

The twentieth century has experienced in the Western Church a great revival in biblical and traditional studies. The Eastern Church and Protest and piety were great factors in this revival. This revival has given to the whole world a more vital and a deeper understanding and love of the liturgical and patristic treasures. The books, studies and scientific research of Western scholars on the Eastern Church's life and liturgical practices are numerous. Because of these studies, the West rediscovered the Fathers of the Church and put back into every hand the spiritual and intellectual wealth that these contain. Here again is another fact to prove how the East needs the West as much as the latter needs the former, and how the two, in humility and truth, make perfect partners in the renewing of the life of humanity in God.

Tradition keeps the Church on the alert, always ready for renewal in strength. It is a leaven always working to "ferment the whole lump." Tradition is continually inspired and sustained by the Holy Spirit. It has a prophetic character, namely, to adapt the Word of God to the times and to the cultures that express the life and mentality of the people of God who live by them. "Indeed, it is the faithfulness to the Fathers as patterns of life in the fullness of the Church, as witnesses to the Mystery in its combined aspects as message, as celebration and as life, that the Church finds her security and looks to the future with confidence" (M.J. LeGuillon, *The Spirit of Eastern Orthodoxy*).

Let us enter into such a marvelous adventure, into this dialogue of God with us, sealed in the covenant.

CHAPTER 5

COVENANT

A COVENANT

Idolatry is not only committed with regard to the nature of God. There is idolatry also in negating our real nature, and especially the essential characteristic of our nature which is freedom. No voice was ever as insistent against idolatry as the voice of Yahweh, God Almighty. No prophet has ever raised a voice as clear sounding as Jesus Christ to champion our freedom and our dignity as free persons before God and others. Where freedom is denied, there is idolatry.

Whenever we bow our heads in blind submission, whenever we remain passive in an abyss of surrender and fear, even in regard to The Law of laws, there is idolatry. Our grandeur is to enter freely with God and with others into a dialogue, a covenant or alliance. Alliance is the expression of the stirring beauty of our being and the deepest reality of our personality as intended and made by God. Freedom is as natural to us (made in the image of God) as it is natural to God himself because he is God.

Of all primitive peoples the Hebrews were the only ones who saw their God as a person, supreme and transcendent; this God still entered into a wondrous mystery of relation with his own creatures. Their God was not the household god of other nations who was considered a protector who himself needed to be protected; or the god of the seasons who presides over the changes of nature. Their God was really the universal Creator. He was the God of history. He made history. He directed all the events of life and gave them a special meaning made them events of salvation: "Now, therefore, if you obey my voice and hold fast to my covenant, you, of all the nations of the earth, shall be my very own, for all the earth is mine" (Exodus 19:5). This is the God Jesus Christ acknowledged and preached, a God of real freedom expressed in a covenant or alliance.

A covenant or alliance is a contract between God and us. In his daily prayer to God, Jesus repeated with his people: "Remember, Yahweh, the covenant, the oath you swore to Abraham!" The covenant is therefore a very special event in the history and existence of our religious life as it was in the life of Jesus Christ and his people. In making a Covenant God proposes the terms and we freely accept or reject them. As free creatures, we can even discuss its terms as did Noah. Once accepted, the contract becomes an alliance that binds us and God, and nothing can invalidate it: "The covenant of God is without repentance." Covenant is a celebration of relation between God and man.

According to the Holy Bible, God made four covenants. The first covenant was made with Noah, the second one with Abraham, and the third with Moses. The fourth and last one was made with humanity, nay with the whole universe in the person of Jesus Christ. This covenant is really a direct relation with God and not a "religion." Each one of these covenants corresponds to a special period of the history of mankind and to the specific needs of humanity for its existence and purpose at that time. Each one constitutes a preliminary clause of a permanent contract where in exchange for his protection and salvation, God requires a certain response or free acceptance which was not asked before. All of these four covenant are complementary and cannot exist without the other.

THE COVENANT WITH NOAH

The first Covenant was concluded with a single individual, Noah, who in reality represented all the descendants who escaped the destruction of the deluge. Noah lives and talks with God, freely, in the name of all races and of all religious beliefs, and even of unbelief. He represents all of them. He represents also all living creatures of the earth, sky, and water. In our modern language we would call such a man "ecumenical." Noah, in the freedom that God recognized and respected in him went as far as to discuss the terms of the covenant: "Do I have to come out of the Ark and start giving birth again to children who, one day, will be wiped out as my contemporaries were?" As long as God did not give his answer, Noah would stay in the Ark with his wife and children and the living creatures with him. God spoke then the promise; "Never again will I curse the earth…As long as the earth lasts, sowing and reaping, cold and heat, summer and winter, day and night shall cease no more" (Gen. 8:21). The signature that sealed this covenant is the Rainbow in the sky.

In his inner life, the Divine Trinity is infinite Celebration. Outside of himself what he created is also a celebration. God confirmed it to be so in this covenant with Noah. Existence is not dormant or static; it is a continual becoming and process. "Sowing and reaping, cold and heat, summer and winter, day and night will ever succeed one after another," said God. Existence vibrates. It sings. It dances. It develops and expands to infinity. Light and love in all directions, it radiates the goodness of its Maker and celebrates him. Creation is a continual celebration.

Our relation with God and with existence is a communication, an interaction and a dialogue of sounds and speech and music and bodily gestures by which our life also becomes a celebration.

The Bible teaches, and Christianity affirms, that each person is created according to the image of God. As Christ is the Image of the Father, and consequently "The High Priest" in creation, so each person being made according to that Image is on the boundary of heaven and earth and therefore, also a priest of God. "Image of God" is not something "added" to our nature or different from it. It is our basic definition and the very essence of our freedom as persons. It is the most intimate aspiration of our being.

Our roots are divine. "Us" means every person, believer and unbeliever, civilized and "uncivilized," just and sinner. In Christian understanding, "there is no Jew or Gentile." Our essential vocation is to be, through our senses and through our minds, priests who celebrate creation. In fact, we do celebrate God when we touch the matter that God created out of his love, the creation which he sanctified and saved through the Incarnation of his Son.

This is the mystery of the union of man with his Creator. This union is first established through our basic contact with the creation. All that exists is God's gift, and it all exists to make God known and to make our life a communion with God. The world is a fallen world because it has fallen away from the awareness that God is ALL in ALL. It is precisely this haughty disregard for God which constitutes the original Sin.

CELEBRATION OF CREATION

Every day the prayerful Christian proclaims in the Creed: "I believe in one God, Creator of heaven and earth, of all things visible and invisible…" In the mouth of the Christian, the word "Creator" means precisely that God is a poet, a life giving artist and a source of life. This is a fact and not an intellectual concept or "doctrine." The Christian proclaims the fact that "God is an artist." To know an artist one has to know his works. The purpose of our life on earth is to be the eyes, the ears, and the conscience of the Creator of the universe. We are the listeners, speakers, and hearers of God's message of love. We are, in one word, priests with a special function which means one thing, and one thing only: the eternal life of God reproduced and realized in the midst of time.

There is absolutely nothing outside God that can possibly necessitate the fullness and richness of his activity to manifest itself outward and grant existence to beings, except the motive of love. In his eternity, in his eternal and infinite movement of love, which is immeasurable and without successiveness, God the Father decides in sovereign freedom to create for his Son, in the Holy Spirit, the whole outward reality as a contingent, finite and so to speak additional source of happiness. He places it in the outer sphere of light and love of the Trinity and confers on it a destiny to return to him and reach him in the sphere of his own light and love. To create the universe, the Father took as a model the perfect image of himself, his Son. The whole creation, therefore, belongs to the Son. He is Pantocrator, and permanent possessor. He united creation to himself in the Incarnation, purified it, redeemed it in his death and resurrection, and graciously brought it back in his Ascension to the Father in the Holy Spirit at Pentecost.

According to Eastern theology, God the Word would have become man in the Incarnation even without the existence of the "felix culpa" (the "happy fault" of Adam), and the historical happening of original sin.

We recognize the Creator in his creation and ultimately we encounter a Father amongst his children. Our celebration is not of an ethical nature, nor is it a mere plea for the preservation or improvement of things in general. It might be that too. But it is first and foremost an experiencing of awe and wonder which draws us to live in an inner fellowship with God. Our experiencing of God's works is a prayer because the experiencing puts our hearts into motion, sighing for and seeking rest in beauty, life, goodness and truth.

Once we have thus seen God, even when we cannot name him, we burst into song, motion, wonder and exaltation. We become a prayer. Many famous poets, artists, and scientist have thus seen God, even though they were often lost for words to name him. "I have noticed through experience and through my own observations that Providence, Nature, God or what I would call the Power of Creation, seems to favor human beings who accept and love life unconditionally. And I am certainly one who does, with all my heart" (Arthur Rubenstein). Rubenstein is lost for words about God. But he has found him in the beauty of art and of life.

Every act inspired by God is creative. The ascetic in the desert, being re created in the divine Light, absorbs the darkness of the earth into his transfigured face. The man of the street who struggles for justice and dignity, the mother who awakens the smile on the face of her child, the lovers who instill the realities of love in each other, all these actions crush the mask of death in order to paint, in light and delight, the face of the Son of God who was made Man so that man can become God.

Let me put his doctrine into theological jargon. In theology we talk about an obscure and impenetrable mystery of God in his creation, his "transcendence" and his "immanence." When we affirm the infinite transcendence we are affirming also the divine immanence. God is so perfectly and infinitely transcendent that even his infinite immanence does not diminish it but, on the contrary, it heightens it. Immanence and transcendence complement each other and fulfill each other. It is possible to say that immanence and transcendence complement each other on the part of the Absolutely simple, Pure Act of the Subsisting Existence itself, God, so that every being becomes consequently the "Diaphany" of God, or the "Transparency" of God. It is like the host at the divine liturgy ready to be divinized. In it we already touch God.

Under the influence of the gospel, our Fathers in the faith, for instance, St. Basil, were proud of the fact that Sophocles, Euripedes, Phedias and other pagan writers and artists were inspired and directed by the Holy Spirit. For them, the works of these artists, philosophers and poets were a blessed and holy liturgy and a witness to the glory of God. The Christian sees in every person's work the glory and awesomeness of God. We stand in religious admiration before every person who applies himself or herself to discover the goodness of God in creation. For the Christian, scientists, artists, workers, organizers and stage performers are holy and sacred. The Christian professes reverence for them, honors their names and blesses their endeavors. The Christian knows that the charisma of their priesthood transforms matter into a form where God shines through. They sing the glory of God. Like "iconographers," they turn the matter of this world towards the light that shines out of the Transfiguration and which transforms it into a new reality worthy of the kingdom. Van Gogh used to say: "I feel like a priest." A Bach cantata spreads a heavenly blessing.

We become what we contemplate. These artists are really contemplating the face of God even if they mistake it for another, or cannot pronounce it, or even if they refuse to recognize it. But the face, the Christian knows, is the face of God. Discipline, self sacrifice, beauty and seriousness of purpose are virtues which link Einstein, Picasso, Rabin-Drana-Tagore, Saint Theresa and Saint Francis to each other and to God. Not every artist is a mystic, but every creative act is a mystical revelation. Every work of art shines with the light of God and each one vibrates with his power and goodness.

The saint sees God in everything

The artist sees God in some things.

The saint vibrates at every touch of the Spirit,

The artist sees only a part of his activity.

The link that unites the artist and the Saint is the Holy Spirit.

They all see God, each one at his or her own level, each according to the gift of God. "Blessed are the pure of heart for they shall see God." The "pure of heart" who saw God are, according to the Gospels, the "adulteress," "the Samaritan woman of five husbands," wicked Zaccheus, the doubting Thomas, the thief and murderer on the cross. These are the Saints of God, the "pure of heart." Being a saint of God is not simply being "moral," but it is living to contemplate God and to be alive in him.

"Blessed are the peacemakers," said the Lord, "for they are children of God." The peacemakers are those who transmit the flame of life, those who experience God and witness to him by transmitting the flame of beauty and enthusiasm. That is what great artists do. They bring us to the realization of the wonders of God and create in us amazement and glorification. The Saints are the flames of God who leave behind them a trail of a special light. When our life is thus fully lived it becomes an immense prayer. The person who has never adored in prayer has never really existed.

THE SPECIAL VOCATION OF THE CHRISTIAN

A Christian is essentially an announcer of good news. His witness to the Gospel blazes everywhere and in everything. His witness consists in recognizing and blessing God's presence and revelation which are more apparent in the life of our modern scientists, artists, poets and creators of social trends than in any other period of the history of mankind.

Besides, we can affirm that the nucleus of all our modern sciences and intellectual and artistic creations was first formed and first developed in religious houses. The first laboratories, the first schools and universities, were created by men of the Church. Many philosophies and modern "isms" were, for good or ill, inspired if not formulated first in the privacy of a monastic cell or in a university run by hooded monks. Our modern world grew from the Church. Later, this same world bypassed her, outgrew her, and negated her. She was too old and too proudly fixed in her human forms and old formulations to be recognized as a creative mother. Her men imprisoned and disfigured her pristine beauty for lust and power. But the Church will shine again and will bring all of humanity back to the unity of life and love and peace which is God.

In 1840 Carlyle wrote as if he were speaking about our own modern times: "In these distracted times, when the religious principle, driven out of most churches, either lies unseen in the hearts of good men looking and longing and silently working there towards some new revelation; or else wanders homelessly over the world, like a disembodied soul seeking its terrestrial organization,…into how many strange shapes of superstition and fanaticism does it not tentatively and errantly cast itself. The higher enthusiasm of man's nature is for the while without exponent; yet does it continue indestructible, unwearily active and at work blindly in the great chaotic deep…" No one who understands the times in which we live can deny that these words sound as if they had been written today.

We cannot exist without God or outside of God. Our real roots are most deeply anchored in an artistic and poetical nature, consequently in religious reality. Our very being entrenches us in God, the "Only Living." Islam proclaims that, "The very first cry of man and his last gasp of breath proclaim the holy Name and pronounce it." The Christian completes this truth by saying, "that every beating of man's heart is basically an act of faith in God."

Magic seeks miracles as exceptional events to upset the ordinary laws of nature. Magic claims power. By the man of God sees that even the ordinary laws of nature are fraught with miracles. He is a man of God who can see the miracle in everything that God has made. When man recognizes the miracle, he naturally and spontaneously bursts into amazement and joy in the artists, performers, in apparently "secularist" people who are religious in the depth of their being.

According to the Christian vision, which was clearly expressed by the Fathers, man, the priest of creation, is to free and save the universe by his activity. He is to "personalize" creation. Other religions, on the contrary, consider that man has to be saved by the universe. For them, it is the universe that gives man his ultimate meaning and raison d'etre by absorbing him into its immensity. For Far-Eastern religions, for instance, man must be absorbed in the impersonal divinity of the universe in order to be saved. He is a prisoner of space and time from which he cannot escape except through patient waiting for the end of life, or by suicide. It is interesting to note that the Chinese people invented gunpowder not to kill or destroy but to play the game of life, to light the skies with firecrackers for their festivities. Orientals also invented games that absorb the greatest amount of time and make man oblivious to life: cards, chess, and all their corollaries. Smoking, for instance, becomes a game of life. The "water pipe" was devised to please, soothe and lull the five senses of man with the fire and the smoke of the tobacco. The smoke makes the water dance and sing. Flowers in the water please the eye. The cool smoke gives a special taste to the mouth. The touch of the pipe is silky or velvety, and the sound of the dancing water fills the ear. On the other hand, Judeo Christians only invented games to improve skills and muscles, or to create a new way of life, or change it again into some other new form. The Judeo Christian, on the contrary, is constantly transforming the world through technology and social reforms. He is a savior and not a prisoner. Mao Zedong had to suppress the basic tenets of China's religion in order to adapt the Judeo Christian attitude and reform his people.

We increase our value and dignity by obeying the order of God to "work" and "subdue the earth." Time is for evolution and re creation and "revolution," and not a spinning wheel on which man is locked and whence he cannot escape except by stoic negation or suicide. This is an arrow that is going somewhere.

St. Denis the Aeropagite describes the universe as an "immense liturgy of sacred dance attracted by a divine Center and gravitating around it." Man is the leader and organizer of the dance and the revealer of its divine meaning. He listens to God and hears an invisible orchestra. He sees man and women circle in the sunbeam of the "One Beyond," and in the scented presence of the "Spirit," and in the trumpeting of the "Resurrection." The organ like notes of creation, the prayerful moaning of the wind, the soft whispering of the waves wheat field, everything in creation makes him sigh and long for that Artist who is God:

> Most honored Paradise,
> garden of beauty and delight,
> dwelling place made perfect by God,
> unending gladness and rejoicing,
> by the harmony of your rustling leaves,
> beseech the Lord Creator
> that He may save our souls.

Nature is fully alive in God. It sways and prays with the person who can listen to the voice of God. Prayer is indeed a listening to that Voice. Creation comes closer to God when it comes closer to itself. It has been said that God is much closer to his creation than creation is to itself. Maximos the Confessor explains that when we have a simple or primary perception of matter we come closer to the Source of being, the Father; when we acquire an analytical knowledge of it, he encounters the Word, the Wisdom of God, the Son; and when we penetrate deep into the complete knowledge of its movement, we soar to the highest degree of our aspiration, to the breath of life, the Holy Spirit. It is precisely through the activity of reason and technology that we bring creation closer to itself and consequently to its source and origin, God. Man is not a conqueror but a lover of creation. Borrowing Paul's language, we can say that the "visible leads man to the Invisible God." And through the beauty and goodness of the creation, God talks back to man.

To really celebrate God in the creation we must first discover the world as though we had never seen it before. We must see the fields covered with lilies, flaming with gladness, the sun and the sky liquids running like a clear river, the earth screaming aloud in delight. To celebrate, one must see the plants, the insects and the innumerable creatures singing aloud with joy. Even a so called "pagan" can enter into such a celebration of God, even when he might not know God's name.

An Egyptian hymn of old Pharos was picked up by David the

prophet, copied and sung in honor of Yahweh. It became psalm 103, a
poem which we, Judeo Christians, consider inspired by God. It has been
sung by Christ and it will be sung forever by Christians and Jews as a
remedy "by which our sins are forgiven us" (St. Basil):

> You are very great, O Lord!
> Clothed in pomp and brilliance,
> arrayed with light as with a cloak.
>
> Stretching out the sky as a tent cloth,
> covering your lofty halls with water.
>
> You make the clouds your conveyance,
> You surge on the wings of the wind.
>
> Down in the gullies,
> You make springs to rise;
> waters shall go down between the mountains.
>
> They shall give drink to the beasts of the field;
> wild asses will seek them to quench their thirst.
>
> You make green pastures for the cattle
> and food plants for the service of man.
>
> So that oil may put a gleam upon his face
> and that bread may strengthen the heart of man.
>
> You have made the moon to mark the seasons;
> the sun knows the time of its setting
>
> Even the wide and open sea itself!
> Within it there are countless creeping things,
> living beings small and large.
>
> Upon it there are ships a sailing
> and that great beast You made to have fun.
> How great are your works! O Lord

in wisdom You have wrought them all

May the Lord's glory be blessed forever,
may the Lord rejoice in his works!

I will sing to the Lord as long as I live,
I will praise my God as long as I last.

And I will rejoice in the Lord.

The realization of the wonders of God in nature makes us enthusiastic, selfless and peaceful. It makes us look to the heart of creation and makes us sing for joy, admiration and awe. The song will purify us and unite us to the Creator. The priesthood of man is a glorious reality.

THE PRIESTHOOD OF MAN IN CREATION

Holy Scripture uses a powerful symbol to describe the priesthood of man and his sublime role of mediator between heaven and earth. The Holy Bible says that God gave Adam the power to confer names. And whatever name he gave to living creatures, "it was so," said God, who thus put his seal on this power of man. Giving a name is indeed an oriental and biblical way of expressing the general priesthood of man, and his intrinsic power as a person, "made in the image and resemblance of God."

According to Greek philosophy and culture, which has blurred Christian vision, a name is only a sound that distinguishes on thing or a person from another. On the contrary, according to the Holy Bible, and to Christ's mentality and culture, a name is much more than a sound. It is a penetration into the essence of a thing or a person. The name denotes a person's very nature and destiny. It tells the value that God assigned to each when he made it. Their value is thus recognized to be God's value, and their worth, God's greatness. To name a person or a thing is to discern and proclaim what God intended it to be, and consequently it is to affirm man's power of it. In fact, a man exercises their power when he gives a name or when he calls someone by name.

God is the first to give names. He gave "Adam," "Abraham," and "Israel" their names. He named prophets, and he named his Son, "Jesus." Christ also gave names to some of his disciples, precisely to manifest his influence over them and give then a new position in life. Simon became "Peter," which means rock. Peter's new relation in life is from now on to be a foundation. It is for this reason one's power over the person or the thing when "called by name" that the Jews could not pronounce the name of God. Moses and the Hebrews could never pronounce "The Name."

To name is also to bless God for his work and to recognize his presence in it. Man is the priest of a Eucharist, offering the world to God, and in this offering he is to receive the gift and fill it with meaning and spirit. To name is to refer the named with all its own natural characteristics and intended value back to its Maker, God, as a glory and as a hymn of praise to him. Only man can recognize the truth, goodness and value of things and establish their relation to God, their author. When one listens to the voice of beauty, he thrills. He is awake. He is conscious of the existence of the Other. It is like a lover who is astonished that someone else exists. St. Francis of Assisi sang songs of glory to the Sun, to his sister Moon, to his sister Water and his brother Fire. Jesus Christ sang songs to the "lilies of the fields, to "the birds of the sky," and to "the growing seed." Only God and man can encounter the other, listen and give a name.

We cannot be too often reminded that there is a God and that this God is an Artist, the greatest of all artists; that he is a Father. As Father, his qualities are reflected in us and in every creature he created. In the power of giving names, man plays his role of priest, performing a holy celebration of life to the honor and glory of his Creator and God. In playing his role of priest and announcer of the goodness of creation, man exercises and affirms his basic and essential characteristic which is freedom. God made an alliance with us and God will always be bound to his word and to his promise; we freely recognize and honor this alliance.

CHAPTER 6

COVENANT WITH ABRAHAM

The second covenant of God was with Abraham. It was not a covenant with the whole of creation like the one with Noah; it was with one person, Abraham and his descendants. The sign and symbol of this covenant circumcision was fixed in the very flesh of man, and marks him for life as belonging to God: "I am El Shaddai…" the God of Abraham. All other gods are fake and false. What a miraculous moment when an unknown man from Mesopotamia became the depositor of the revelation of the oneness and uniqueness of God! This revelation will be the starting point of a new history of mankind. The free alliance of God and man is signed, on the part of man, with circumcision, which seals man as belonging to God. On the part of God is the promise of a special nation who will occupy a special land, a "Promised land."

Nationhood means, for all peoples of the earth, living in one place. Abraham and his descendants, after this covenant, emerge as a nation long before they could call any soil their own. Abraham, who was to become a nation, was a wanderer. He died a wanderer. His generations after him were wanderers. Jacob and his twelve children all died as wanderers in a strange country. Moses and all the people he led out of Egypt were wanderers. They also died wandering in the desert.

It is the moral strength and the glory of the people of the covenant that they were born in time, not in a place. The "Promised Land" was the sign of the faithfulness of God and the guarantee of this covenant. It is precisely for this reason that it is called the "Land of the Holy." It really belongs to God in a very special way because it is the land of his covenant.

Through the history of the people of Israel, we can clearly see that

God disposes of the land they occupy according to their response to the covenant, God sends collapse, military defeat and national destruction. He takes his land away and sends his unfaithful people into exile. When they keep the covenant and remain loyal to God, the land is theirs and prosperity reigns supreme.

The Children of Abraham have been emigrating willingly or unwillingly for centuries. In their Diaspora they encountered dispersion and peace, favorable rulers and persecutors, tolerance and death, safety and terror and panic. They always found themselves a disturbing minority among strong and suspicious majorities. Some of them acquired, in Nordic countries, a skin as white as almond blossom. Some became brown and black in the heat of the desert. But as a "people," as a special community, they never dissolved. They were depositors and witnesses of the uniqueness of One-ness of God.

The miracle of this people is that they have lasted all through the centuries against all human opposition and all human odds of survival. The history of mankind's emigration is clear to all. No people on earth ever emigrated to another human family without being swallowed up by it, sooner or later. Being an encumbrance, minorities are dissolved into the majorities they join. Thus, Greeks, Romans, Arabs and Asians, Syrians and Turks, became through a slow process of amalgamation, French, German, Russian or American. If some genetic traits did not dissolve, the traits remained only as a reminder of one's origin. A Swede in America, or an Italian in France, bear witness to their physical origin. And this is the extent of their differences. Not so with the people of the Promise.

I do not maintain that there was no compromising among the Jews. Assimilation carried away such a great number of them that they sometimes felt that no one would be left to carry on the people. Yet, a small remnant remained; Judaism renewed its youth from the ashes of the dead. This is Judaism's answer to the mystery of its uniqueness. Everywhere, small or great, weak or strong, they were a people destined "to return." The Creator himself had promised the return. God is faithful to his promise.

Thus we can understand that the historical experience of the Jewish people is a unique human phenomenon. Dispersed among nations, they never entirely dissolved. They always kept alive their relation with the God of Abraham. They kept the originality of their faith and their undaunted faithfulness to their traditions: They were everywhere a community. Only rugged individuals can form a community.

The historical experience of the Jews is that they always formed a community. Abraham started a community. The twelve children of Jacob Israel went down to Egypt to form a community. They came back to Canaan to form a community. Moses and the Torah sealed them as a community, a family whose members were responsible for each other. All through their three thousand years of peregrinations, and long before Christ and long after him, they formed communities.

The twelve Apostles of Christ who were all Jews were a community. All those who followed these Apostles formed communities. Even Gentiles who joined them learned from the Jewish people how to form a community. The unity of this people as intended by God in his promise to Abraham, and of the communities they formed, where each belongs to all and all to each, is clearly stated in the Talmud: "If any man caused a single soul to perish from Israel, Scripture imputes it to him as though he has caused a whole world to perish; but if any man saves a soul from Israel, Scripture imputes it to him as though he has saved the life of a whole world."

Wherever Jewish communities were established, their special destiny was to "Reveal," and to "Witness." The Hebrew word "Galouth"-dispersion, diaspora-means also "revelation." They were dispersed to reveal. They could not dissolve into other nations. Through time and space, their experience as a group, as a community, was and still is to reproduce life consonant with the life of the Creator, to witness to God and to a Mystery beyond human comprehension.

The story of Creation itself is an alliance between God and his people, the Jewish people, preparing for Jacob, Israel. The story of Abraham was a story of a revelation of God's presence and a response of man to his God. This same revelation became, between man and God, and alliance, a "covenant."

With Moses the covenant became law and hierarchy. With the Prophets, the law became a vision of peace, justice and goodness, and a cosmic law of the freedom of the children of God. This was the real promise. This was the stamp of God on his people, the Jews, who thus represent humanity. Even in the longest and most destructive of all their exiles, the Jews never died out. They were rather purified for a progressive realization of the salvation history and of the intention of God which was to set them up as a blessing for all nations (Gen. 12). They were always promised the "Return." God always kept his promise. Their return from Babylon, for instance, proved to be, according to Symeon, the priest of the temple of Jerusalem, "A light of revelation to the Gentiles, and the glory of the people of God, Israel" (Luke 2:32).

On the surface, the land of the promise is like any other land of the world. It is not Genesis, or the delight of Eden found and lost, nor the Voice thundering from beyond the clouds that lends it the fascination that it has on every human heart. Every corner of the earth ahs had its paradise. Each has beheld the mystery of life and the groaning of its painful development. It Is not the swamps or the deserts of the South, nor the hills and valleys of Galilee or of Judea that gripped the heart of Israel in Exile and made them long, long and sigh, with tears, for the return.

Everywhere in the world Jews have had homes and palaces and the best of human possessions and knowledge. Furthermore, wherever their eyes have turned to settle and live, they excelled in all the endeavors possible to man. They produced inventors, musicians, artists, industrialists and creators of thought hat changed the face of the earth. There is Moses, Christ, Paul, Marx, Engels, Freud, Einstein and Picasso, to cite but a few among a host of others. Their longing and fascination for their land do not spring from a desire for land as much as a yearning for a "home," a home which radiates a very special quality: that of a "family" where an encounter of love can be realized. Their longing is for a Person who identified himself with this land, for the shalom of a security that has no shadow. "Peace I leave you; my peace I give to you; not as the world gives do I give to you. Let not your hearts be troubled, neither let them be afraid" (Jn 14:27). These are the words of a real Jew talking to full blooded Jews and to all their generations.

To each tribe of Israel God gave a piece of land; to Levi, he gave none. He rather wanted himself to "be their lot!" Nazareth is not a mere geographic town but a place identified with a Person. It is in Nazareth that God Beauty took a human face and where God Love became a human heart. It is the place where the Infinite became a human heart. It is the place where the Infinite became finite and where the womb of a Jewish girl from the house of David became his throne and the glory of womanhood. The Christian religion holds this to be a sure fact that in Nazareth God became a Jewish Man, so that all men can become God. The longing for the return, then, is not merely the longing for some barren soil but, in Christian eyes, a yearning for an encounter with that Person, Christ.

For us Christians, Bethlehem is not only the town of David, the Prophet and poet. It is the place where heaven joined earth, where angels learned from the Jewish people how to sing and dance, where the Invisible could be seen in a human face. Christ came to reveal the Father, Yahweh himself. The longing was not for the Torah but for a Person, not for a code but for Love, for the Infinite love of God manifested in the Jew, Jesus Christ. What the people of God could not see without dying "None can look at my face and live," said the Lord to Moses now became a Jewish face, a brother's face, a lover's smile, "one like unto any other Jew" (St. Paul). The yearning for the return is not the yearning for a piece of land, but a yearning to see that face of love and "not die."

Jerusalem and Galilee are not mere hills surrounded with deserts or lush green valleys. They are centers of life and love permeated with the activities of the "Son of David, Son of Abraham, Son of God." It is in Jerusalem that this Son of God, the Jew of Jews, wrought and accomplished the salvation of the human race. In him, the people of Israel spread their wings to cover the whole universe. In him, the people of Israel became the benefactors of all mankind. From now on, because of the people of Israel, blessing can always flow upon humanity. In him, the Christ, and by him, the God of Abraham became known as the God of the whole universe. Jerusalem is now the real "navel of the world." It is only in Jerusalem that Christ offered himself in his Jewish flesh and blood, as a sacrifice for the salvation of Jews as well as of Gentiles. The fascination of the land is not in soil and stones, but in the mysterious attraction to see his face which is imprinted in the very atmosphere of the Land. Jerusalem! "Next year in Jerusalem!" This is the covenant God made with Abraham.

By the "return of the Jews" I am not claiming that every individual Jew had to dwell in the Land of the Holy. The Diaspora, or Galouth, as I have already explained, has to go on, along with the Christian witness, among all nations in all its spiritual and human dimensions. It has to continue to witness to God, to humanity and to the salvation history of mankind. "Galouth" means "dispersed to witness." "It is therefore the lot of the Jews to live and suffer and serve in glory, in their old identity until the day, promised by God, when his name will be one in all the earth and all nations glorify him in one accord" (Herman Wouk). The Christians call "that day" the "Parousia."

In the whole of the Sacred Tradition which we hold in common with our ancestors the Jews and our brothers the Muslims, space is a human reality into which God has entered in order to meet man and reveal his presence and his will. At the oak of Mamre near Shechem, the patriarch Abraham was visited by the Lord who made him the primes of the land: "So Abram built an altar there to the Lord who appeared to him" (Gen. 12:7).

This rhythm of appearance oracle worship is repeated in many places in the Bible and reaches its greatest exemplification in the building of the Temple. The many great kindnesses which the Lord had shown to David were brought to a culmination when, in response to David's intention to build a house for the Lord, Nathan received this oracle for David: "Are you the man to build me a houses to dwell in? I will provide a place for my people Israel...The Lord will make you great, the Lord will make a house for you..." (2 Sam. 7:5-16).

Certain places have a special power for Jews and Moslems. Their importance derives from the fact that those who visit them are purified and made holy. Visits to such places are an essential part of their worship, as is well known. Going to the Temple is a basic requirement for the completion of a Jewish man's prayer, and is a necessary step whenever possible in the achievement of salvation.

In Islam, the pilgrimage first to Mecca and Madeena, and then later to the Al Aska Mosque in Jerusalem, is one of the five pillars of the religion. This Pilgrimage, again, whenever possible, is of real necessity for a Moslem who desires the completion of his religion and the security of his salvation.

We Christians, however, do not have such pillars of our faith. There is no necessity for us to visit a special place or temple or shrine; we are not obliged to go on pilgrimage, not even to Jerusalem! Even the word ekklesia in the New Testament, as is well known, never refers to a building. It refers to the gathering of believers who in their mutual love and their prayer to God not only realize the gahal gathered in the desert to hear the word of he Lord, but also make present once again the reality of the risen Lord Christ Jesus. Jesus promised his disciples that "where two or three meet in my name, there I am in their midst" (Matt. 18:19-20). This is our Christian belief, and fidelity to it would not only heal us of our excessive attachment to splendid buildings and rich ornaments, but it would free us to reverence the beliefs of our brothers, the Moslems and the Jews, and to rejoice in the way that God treats them.

The Gospel tells us that when Jesus entered the Temple he was distraught by the lack of reverence for the sacredness of the place. When he drove out the buyers and sellers and money changers, he was challenged and asked for a sign of his authority. He replied: "Destroy this temple and in three days I will raise it up." The Gospel goes on to explain, "Jesus was speaking of the temple of his body" (John 2:19-21). This is the view of the Christian faith: The Body of Christ is the new Temple from which flow rivers of living water (Ezech. 47:1, Zech. 14:8; Jn. 7:38-39); it is the sanctuary wherein dwells the Shekina (Jn. 1:14). But this Body of Christ is not only the Body of Jesus. It is that physical Pleroma or fullness which the believers make up as united to Jesus Christ.

This does not mean that we despise place as a means of entering into contact with God; nor is it that we are superior to others by being "spiritual" while others are "material" or "earth bound" (what is more "material" than our belief in the Incarnation!). We Christians believe that the promise made to David, that God would build him a house, a dynasty, is ultimately realized in Jesus who with his Body makes up what Paul calls the Temple of God, the place where pure hands should be raised in intercession for all men in praise of the God and Father of Our Lord Jesus Christ: "Didn't you realize that you were God's temple and the Spirit of God was living in you? If anybody should destroy the temple of God, God will destroy him, because the Temple of God is sacred; and you are that Temple" (1 Cor. 3:16-17).

Place is still sacred to us, but we have become that place. When the Samaritan woman asked Jesus where the correct place of worship was to be found, he replied: "Believe me, woman, the hour is coming when you will worship the Father neither on this mountain nor in Jerusalem. God is spirit, and those who worship must worship in spirit and in truth" (Jn. 4:21-24).

If we were to take this seriously, then we would truly live by the Spirit of God and freely respect the beliefs of the Jews who, ever since their exile in Babylon, have greeted on another on their feast days and on other occasions with the expression of their dearest wish: "Ba Shana ha ba Yerushalaym! Next year Jerusalem!" At a Jewish wedding, the bridegroom takes a glass and breaks it, repeating with the psalmist, "If I forget thee Jerusalem, let my right hand wither, let my tongue cleave to the roof of my mouth…" (Ps. 137:5-6). Jerusalem for the Jews is the symbol of their very existence as a nation and a religion under God. It is the place in which they struggle and compete for the honor of possessing a few feet of ground in which their bodies can be placed at their death. When it comes to Jerusalem there is no difference between an Orthodox, a Reformed, a Conservative, a Liberal, or even a unbelieving

Jew! Jerusalem is the Zion of God, and no Jew disputes this. When a well known socialist Jewish leader was asked why, as a non believing Jew, he was so tenaciously attached to Jerusalem he answered: "When it comes to Jerusalem, we're all religious."

The Jew believes that the Holy City of Jerusalem is the center of the world. Each and every Jew bows his head in respect and devotion when he stands by the Western (wailing) Wall. In that place, all Jews are united in God's love. All their differences melt away and disappear. As they stand there together, God's love and their common history blends them into one, and all grudges, hatreds, disputes, differences of religious outlook or political view are forgotten. The place works its effect on them. God is dwelling among them.

The same thing can be said of the Moslems when they go to the Mosque of Al Aqsa. There they are reminded of the pilgrimage of their Prophet Mohammed to this very spot. The story is told of an angel of the Lord who brought Mohammed to the place where there now stands the Mosque of Al Aqsa. Some interpreters say that this is an actual happening; others that it was a vision in a dream by which God wished to show the importance of Jerusalem for the completion of the Moslem's religion. The Mosque in Jerusalem is considered by Islam to be the third Holy Place after Mecca and Medina. It is sufficient once to have seen the crowds gathered in that Mosque and all around it, and at the Dome of the Rock, to experience how, for Moslems, this is a moment of entering into the "fear of the Lord." The people at prayer melt together in a unity of praise. Their very presence in this holy place fills their hearts with awe and a sense of God's presence under whose wings all find equal refuge and equality with one another. Here God revels all the splendor of his glory that can be perceived in this life. The place becomes a source of unity and love. God is seen among his people.

I will speak later about the beauty of the Holy Land for the Christian believer. Here I wish of all to ask a question about the very nature of our presence in the Holy City.

What has our so called devotion to the holy places of the Gospel done for ourselves and for the witness we are meant to give to the world? Isn't it true that most of the story of our presence there is marked by wars and bloodshed, by disputes and wrangling, by political maneuvering and jealous attachment! While we are so busy fighting, especially with one another, don't we bring shame and disgrace on the name of Christ, whose presence and suffering and death and resurrection is the only reason that we can call these places holy at all? Jesus came to preach a message of love and peace, and we are so busy worrying about places that we forget what he came to teach us; we make others forget it too.

But the problem is deeper, I think. Doesn't the fact that the holy places of our religion serve to divined us rather than unite us, as the holy places of the Jews and the Muslims unite them, prove to us that we do not take seriously the fact of our faith? Where is the sacred space where Christ meets the believer? It is in the assembly of the community wherever that community meets in his name. Wherever Christians meet in love for one another and for all others in union with Jesus, there is the place of the Resurrection. The whole point of our religion is that the tomb is empty! Why do we fight over it?

Jerusalem is a mysterious magnet, attracting the hearts of Christians believers from all over the world. But what we see there now is not one Mother Church. We do not see the marvelous unity of love that embraces variety, in which each one is proud of the achievements of his brothers.

We rather see groups of people afraid of each other, reflecting and enhancing the divisions that are the scandal of Christianity the world over. We see people fighting over a place near the Holy Sepulcher where they can put their candlestick. It is not only that we shock people by our attachment to a place; deeper than that, we have misunderstood the very role of place in the Christian faith, and our responsibility for making place, any place, holy.

We know from our tradition that the first Christians built shrines at the places they identified with incidents in the life of Christ. It is significant that in nearly all these places, what was built was a place of prayer, not a place of liturgical cult. Under the influence of Roman Empire and the pagan factors present in it, enthusiasm for the places which had known the presence of Christ underwent the influence of magical ideas. Some of these ideas are with us yet, and it should be the duty of the shepherds of the Church to heal their flocks of these notions even at the risk of losing some financial support for the shrines.

What I am saying is this: the pilgrimages as we know them today are a counter witness to the simplicity, the spirituality, the poverty, the sincere love taught by the Gospel. The jealousy with which each Christian group guards and promotes its shrines or its part of a shrine is exactly the opposite of the message being given out by the bell sounding in the tower of a Church with a cross on its top, calling people to prayer, not to some blind, magical instinct that their mere presence in a place will confer some benefit on them.

The fact of our disputes and arguments over what we consider holy ought to make us reconsider what we have become used to calling our "rights" in the Holy Land. If we cannot make the exercise of these "rights" bring people to a deeper union with Christ and with one another, then we should give up these "rights," yielding them up for the sake of others. If the Church is to be truly Catholic, that is Universal, then it must give up those things that make it small and narrow and cause others to become the same. The Church must abide by the injunction of Jesus: "If your right eye should cause you to sin, tear it out and throw it away" (Mt. 5:28). If something in the life of the Church is causing it to sin, it must be torn out and thrown away.

CHAPTER 7

COVENANT WITH MOSES

The third covenant of God was made in the Sinai desert. The Sages and Hebrews commentators of the Torah point out that this covenant was a universal covenant. It belongs to all the nations of the earth. They explain that it was made in a desert so that no one nation, not even the nation of Israel, could claim it as an exclusive possession. "As no nation can possess a desert," they said, "no nation can claim exclusively for itself what happens in a desert." Moses on the mountain was only an interpreter of God's will to the people and the ambassador of a whole people with God. Inspired by God, Moses passed on to the people and to their descendants the vision that God was the Creator of heaven and earth, and that he will always remain their personal creator and God. He was the greatest and most powerful among the gods of all nations.

Moses instilled also in his people the will of this Creator and God. Their destiny was to be teachers and a blessing for all mankind because they were the witnesses of his uniqueness and of his concern and care for humanity. If they remained faithful to him the world will come to know him as a Savior. One cannot separate the history of mankind from the history of salvation. The history of salvation is that everything converges towards God. He is the beginning and the end of all the events that surround mankind. The history of salvation of mankind is in Jesus Christ, and in his people, the Jews, and this very history will go on in them until "all the Gentiles come in…" (Rom. 11:25).

THE SABBATH

This whole exalted vision of creation, salvation and the mission of the people of Israel as a blessing to mankind was sealed by God and Moses in the observance of the Sabbath. The Sabbath is the seal of the partnership of God and man in their rule of creation and of man's destiny. It is man's participation in the goodness of God's creation, the affirmation and joyous acceptance of the world created by God as good: "And God saw it was good! And God blessed it!" (Gen. 1:25).

Having lived through six days filled with work and relaxation, suffering and joy, hatred and love, man looks for an oasis of rest. He needs to take stock. The sight of birth and death, of success and failure, of the loved and unloved, the lonely and the abandoned, of the brutal and the compassionate, haunts him. Man needs a sustaining hope and a meaning to life. God instituted the Sabbath to be that oasis which would furnish that fresh outlook on creation, man and God.

Moses and Israel accepted the offer of God. The Sabbath is not therefore an ordinary work stoppage. Its essence is participation in the delight and sacredness of divine peace found in the goodness of space and time. If the world is a time of sin, exile and alienation from God, the Sabbath will point to a new day of salvation, redemption and resurrection. It will bring to mind the final triumph of the Kingdom of God. Furthermore, the Sabbath, for Jews in our time, is the day of the messianic era, a foretaste of the coming peace between man and God, man and nature, man and man. It is a day of ennobling pleasure.

Negatively, it forbids all acts, even the most effortless, that contain an element of innovation, or of workmanship. Traditions stemming from Mosaic times list thirty-nine banned labors covering the basic pursuits of men: bread, clothing, shelter, meat and leather, manufacture, and commerce. Negative as it seems to be, this outlook takes on a dramatic ceremony penetrating all of life. Religious ceremony aims, like art, at the shock of truth. The Sabbath ceremony aims at the meaning of the destiny of Israel; it is a seal that cuts deep into Jewish life. Looming so large in life, coming so often, the Sabbath has a lifetime in which to imprint its meanings on the spirit and on the brain. Those who keep it will inevitably imbibe the ideas of creation, of the Creator, of the Exodus, and of Jewish identity. Those who do not keep it miss something of the necessary meaning of their identity. As long as man does not return to his roots, to the humus of his ground of being, all reforms are but masks.

"The Sabbath is a Bride, and nightfall the wedding hour, so that every Friday at dusk pious Jews red the sparkling love poetry of the Songs of Songs" (H. Wouk). There dawns an awareness that God's love and God's bounty and tenderness are real and true.

For more than three centuries, Christianity observed the Sabbath.

Sunday was not even a day of rest. It was called "fixed day": "They gathered on a fixed day." Through that one day, all days, all times were transformed into times of remembrance and expectation.

The covenant concluded on Mount Sinai offered the people of Israel a law, and the people responded by pledging fidelity to its obligation, along with fidelity to the sanctity of the Sabbath observance. The crowning glory of this Covenant is that the people of Israel were charged with a divine mission and given as a blessing to mankind. Confident in this sublime mission and in the goodness and generosity of God to his people, Moses asked to see the face of God: " 'You cannot see my face,' answered God, 'No man can see me and stay alive; you can see only the back of me, but my face is not to be seen…'" The fourth covenant in Jesus Christ will be the covenant of the Face, where man can look at the face of God and not die.

It was neither the vision alone, nor the law that made the unconquered greatness of the Jews. It was the mystery of their witness and the meaning of their being the people of the Covenant of God. A mystery is always close, within the reach of the hand, and yet so far away; so near and clear, and yet, beyond human understanding. That is what the covenant of God is a miracle of survival, a miracle of beauty and of witness that will attain the summit of perfection in Christ who is the Cosmic Witness to the universal stirring of freedom, joy and fulfillment.

The Jewish people, as people of the covenant of God, are therefore, a symbol, pointing to a reality beyond all human realities and all human understanding. It points to the uniqueness of God. A symbol is not make believe, or a mere sign. It is reality distilled. A Jew might be religious, a religious, or irreligious; he is yet stamped with something special, something so beautifully beyond human expectation that he inspires awe, indignation, or wonder. He points to God, and to the fulfillment of all his promises in Jesus Christ.

All historic moments of humanity are rocked either by hope or by despair. Men are either lulled by promises or stirred by prophecies. They live in expectation. They are stirred by the inexplicable, and they wonder. They want to explain and understand, and often they feel powerless. Despite all their intellectual efforts, they feel that they are groping in darkness, especially when they touch the things of the Spirit. Many are the mysteries that surround us and make us wonder. One of these mysteries has, for centuries, been plaguing many historians, sociologists, lawyers, and politicians, both within the people of Israel and outside it.

It is the question: "What is a Jew?" This question mystifies Synagogues and Christian Churches alike. It is still dangling, like a sword of Damocles, in the Knesset of the State of Israel today, in its courtrooms, and in the hearts of us all.

What is a Jew? Is it the fact that one has come from the loins of Abraham? Or is it the mere fact of worshiping the God of Abraham and following his law given at the hands of Moses? Is it faithfulness to the Talmud; or could it be some other legal reality or fiction? The Christian world is as much interested and involved in this question as the Jews themselves. Christ was a Jew; the first Christians and the first disciples and followers of Jesus Christ were Jews; and all the Apostles were Jews.

If being a Jew were a reality like any other reality, it would have been defined and explained. Besides, after thirty-five hundred years of continuous history, one would think that a people would have worked out a handy definition of their identity! But being a Jew is a reality of the spirit; it needs special consideration and attention. It needs the eyes of the soul, the eyes of angels, the eyes of God to see and understand it. All human intellectual powers can hammer at the question. They will crack the shell. The kernel is a mystery and a beauty that no human eye or legal definition can penetrate.

No system of thought or rational analysis can ever give the whole truth about a person, a people. How much more elusive is the miraculous endurance of the Jewish people through centuries of persecution!

What is a person? What is a people? What is a personal or spiritual relation? These are realities that cannot be completely explained. Systems of thought can touch something of the reality but not all its inner richness and substance can be revealed. Indeed, unless we go beyond the visible, we never know very much about real reasons, about meanings, about the future, or about why we are always reaching beyond ourselves. Only through contemplation and prayer, with the help of reason, can we see and understand the whole truth.

How many Christians, throughout two thousand years of existence, have prayed on their knees to the God of Abraham, Moses, and David, the God of Jesus Christ, and asked to have the eyes of the angels, the eyes of the soul, to see and understand the love which seals the "people of the Promise," the Jewish people? Many Christians have always recognized in the Jewish people a special mission, a light and a beauty that no human reality can surpass or even equal. The Jews were entrusted with the witness to God and to his salvation.

It is through the covenant that the belief in one God has entered the world and has been inscribed in the heart of mankind. Judaism is the starting point of Christianity on the one hand, and of Islam on the other. Christianity owes Israel its very essence: Christ, the Apostles, the bible and all its riches all flow from Judaism, Islam also owes Judaism its essence, which is the unity of God, the law that binds to God and neighbor, and circumcision.

The Jews are special witnesses, not only to God, but specifically to cosmic salvation. "Emmanuel," the Messiah, the Promised, the Anointed of God, the Sent, Son of Abraham, Son of David comes from the very essence, and is at the very heart and fiber of Israel. In the reality of the Spirit, he is "The Emmanuel," the Image and Revealer of God, God of God, the Savior of mankind. Jesus Christ is one and unique reality wedded in one divine Person, the Word of God made man. To witness to such a savior is the most exalted, and at the same time, the most bewildering witness to a truth that is beyond intellectual human grasp, yet so real and so true.

For us Christians, Christ is the Emmanuel. He is the image and Word of God, Yahweh. As Image of God, Christ is one with God. We believe that when this Son of God became man he brought God to man. And as man he united man and all of humanity to Yahweh, God himself. He bridged the abyss that separates creatures from the Creator. A Christian, therefore, is the one who believes that in Christ he receives the covenant of God made not only with Noah but also with Abraham, with Moses and with the Prophets. In our baptism into Christ, Christians believe that they are clothed with the justice of God and with the love of God which contains the whole Law and the Prophets.

By these affirmations, we Christians do not intend to suppress, change or negate the Jews' religious experience and religious convictions. We are simply giving testimony to a fact, the testimony which we have received from a dazzling array of witnesses, specifically Jewish witnesses, the Apostles and first Christians who were all Jews. Consequently, we do not intend any offense to Jews who did not accept the message of Christ, a Jew from their very flesh and blood. Besides, it is a testimony of a formidable intellectual position with which most of the first class minds of the human race, Christian as well as non Christian, century after century, have concurred.

Did this Messiah really come, or is he yet to come? Some Jews said he did come. They "saw him." They "touched him." They "ate with him." "We have found the Messiah!" (John 1:41). They recognized in him all that the Law and the Prophets had foretold: "We have found him of whom Moses in the Law, and the Prophets, wrote, Jesus of Nazareth, the Son of Joseph" (John 11:45). The testimony of those Jews, direct descendants of Abraham and faithful disciples of Moses, is a simple testimony, clear, seeking no personal gain or glory.

After having "found him" they lived with him three long years. They experienced his unbounded love, his extraordinary way of witnessing to Yahweh, "My Father," as he called him. They were convinced beyond the shadow of any doubt that he was the promised Messiah. They laid down their lives to profess their conviction. They gave their testimony, compelled by their conscience, their experience, and by their great love for God and for his people Israel, their own people. This conviction and testimony were received with the same conviction by other Jews and others who later on followed them and accepted their preaching were called by the name "Christian." Outsiders and onlookers pagans dubbed them with this name, because their conviction and their testimony for Christ were deeply rooted in their Jewish religious and social life.

To be a Christian, therefore, is to accept the Messiah Jews themselves preached to the world. To be a real Christian is to commit and dedicate one's self not to a Book but to a Person from the Jewish race; not to a Law but to that very Person who is the Image of God Yahweh, God of God, and at the same time real man of the Jewish flesh and blood who lived and died in his own Jewish historical context.

Are those who did accept such a message from Jews in a Jewish language and mentality to be rejected by the other Jews who did not accept the message? By no means! If anyone is to blame for such an acceptance, it is those who put forward the message, not those who accept it.

Other Jews did no accept the claims of Jesus and the preaching of their own co religionists about Jesus. Yet, they had heard and touched and experienced the same Christ as the latter. These were rather shocked and offended when Jesus suggested: "If you abide in my word...you shall know the truth, and the truth shall make you free..." (John 8:32). They believe they already possessed the truth and therefore they were free. Their zeal, their genuine desire to live according to the Law of Moses, prevented them from accepting the Word of Jesus and following him. To them, salvation was found only in the practice of the Law. They were expecting a Messiah with more of a political message.

Are these Jews who did not accept the message of Christ to be ostracized or despised by those who did? St. Paul has the answer: "You, my brothers [who followed Christ], should know that my heart's desire and prayer to God is for them [the Jews who did not follow]. They have not accepted the message of freedom and salvation, but they still are the Chosen Ones, the Beloved of God. I ask then, has God rejected his people? By no means" (Rom. 10:11). Paul is so overturned by the grandeur of the calling of his people that he comes back again and again to this same idea and conviction: "I say then, God has not rejected his people, has he? May it never be! But by their transgression salvation has come to the Gentiles, to make them jealous. Now if their transgression be riches for the world, and their failure riches to the Gentiles, how much more will their fulfillment be!" (Rom. 11:25).

I would here recommend that every Jew and Christian read and learn by heart Chapter Eleven of St. Paul to the Romans. The Jews will find in it a Jew who is uncovering the real meaning of his Jewishness in his relation to Christ; for the Christians, it is a reminder of how they should look at their own origin as Christians. The Jews at the time of Jesus, like the Jews of our day, like the Jews who will carry their Jewishness into eternity, are and will remain the people who are carrying in their flesh and blood that "hope and future" promised by God, and who will forever represent the "One we have found" (John 1,4). We respect and honor their position. We are full of admiration and love. Not paternalistic, condescending love but genuine, profound and sincere love given to a real flesh and blood brother.

The Christian religion believes and teaches the truth of Jesus Christ which is primarily love. No Christian can approach the altar or celebrate God if he harbors rancor or hatred against anyone. But the sad fact is that Christians have been approaching all the altars of the world with a heavy conscience and uneasy step. They had a certain hate in their hearts against their won kin, the Jews, caricatures and comparisons that are not worthy of their origin. They often said that the Jews were the killers of Christ, and consequently guilty, and should be a target for revenge.

This allegation has been declared by the bishops of the world as a theological, historical and juridical error. On October 28, 1965, the Second Vatican Council promulgated the famous and controversial declaration *Nostra Aetate,* in which, among other things, the Church recalls that, according to the teaching of the New Testament, she has been nourished by the "roots of the natural olive tree" which is the Jewish people, and on which the branches of the "wild olive tree, the Church of the Gentiles have been grafted" (Rom. 11). This declaration was only a beginning to lead the Christians to understand better their faith, the teaching of Christ, and to create a brotherly atmosphere of mutual respect and love, if possible, between Christians and Jews (*Nostra Aetate* 4,2).

This declaration of the Council has in all Christian countries and communities, been explained, accepted and publicized by theologians, and by official local authorities. The French Episcopal Commission made public a great statement in 1973. On January 3, 1975 Pope Paul of Rome sent again a message *Urbi et Orbi* (for Rome and the world) in the same spirit. His was immediately followed by an official declaration and endorsement by the American hierarchy, asking all Christian to complement, by word and deed, such declarations.

The biggest problem that makes Christians and Jews clash is nourished as vividly and deliberately by Jews against Christians as by Christians against Jews. Jews taught each other and their children to hate and condemn Jesus who is considered to be the apostate par excellence; and to hate Christians because they followed a Jewish apostate and because they persecuted Jews. It is naïve and unhistorical to think that Jews disliked Christians merely because naughty Christians first hurt innocent Jews. A world of hypocrisy has been created in Christian churches as well as in synagogues, a world which speaks of religious or social values on the one hand, while destroying the "individual and his dignity, on the other, and thus effacing in him the likeness of God." "Race of hypocrites!" These words of Christ are applicable to all of us. It is high time for all of us, Christians as well as Jews, to pull down our masks and our defense mechanisms. We should look at each other as a real family of brothers.

Most Jews believe, as many Christians unfortunately still believe, that Christ was against the Jews, against the Law of Moses, against the Talmud and the Jewish tradition. These people still think that the New Testament teaches hatred and discrimination against Jews. Some ill-intentioned or misguided writers have gone so far as to snip out of the New Testament some criticism made by Jews against their own kind. These same writers have collected some of the words of the New Testament or some vague expressions which sound harsh and strong. They have strung them together, and offered the results to Jews and to Christians as the true face of the Christian reality vis-à-vis the Jews. If we had to apply the same technique to the Old Testament and especially to the Talmud, even to the most beautiful and holy writings of the Hasidim vis-à-vis the Christians and non Jews, one could also produce a horrible picture of the Jews, as a blood thirsty and racist people who hate everyone who is not of Jewish blood.

It is true that Paul, John and the other Jewish apostles criticized the "the Jews." But they themselves were Jews. They could criticize their own; but they never accepted any criticism from anyone else. "If some of the branches were broken off and you [who became Christians], a wild shoot, were grafted in their place to share with them the richness of the olive tree, do not be arrogant toward the branches [the Jews]. But if you are arrogant, remember that it is not you who support the root [the Jewish people] but the root supports you" (Rom. 11:17sq.).

According to the best biblical scholars, it must be admitted also that Jesus' controversies with some religious leaders of his time, called in the Gospels "the Jews," are colored by the apologetic interests of the early Church which was frequently in conflict with Judaism and persecuted by it. The first Christians were hated by the synagogue, despised and condemned by their own. They were jeered and mocked and smeared in the popular mind as "traitors," "child killers," "donkey worshipers," "lechers," "cowards." They were ever ready scapegoats for public ire and persecution. Their own Jewish brothers delivered them to Roman jailers to be imprisoned and killed.

"The Jews" were, therefore, to some extent, the enemies of Christians and of the New Testament writers, and for that reason those writers are less than fair to the deeper Jewish spirituality of the time of Jesus. There were indeed Pharisees, who were blinded by narrow nationalistic prejudices and stifled by petty legalism. But there were others who were men of noble character and genuine piety who worshiped God sincerely and loved their neighbors "expecting nothing in return" (Luke 6,35). The contrast between Jesus and the Pharisees, therefore, was also exaggerated by these writers.

The overall picture captured in the New Testament is rather awesome in its esteem and love for the people of God as a religious nation and as a race. Christ himself was very conscious of being a Jew, so much so that he treated Gentiles as "dogs" in comparison with the children of his Jewish people. The word "dog" applied to a person was, and still is in the Eastern mentality and language, the supreme insult and a most despising expression. Christ threw the word right in the face of a defenseless Gentile woman: "It is not good to take the children's bread and throw it to the dogs" (Matt. 15:21-27, Mark 7:24-30). On the contrary, his most cherished compliment is to call someone "son or daughter of Abraham." He rewarded with an astounding miracle a Roman Centurion, a pagan, because the latter had built a synagogue for his people.

This same Jesus was born according to the Law of Moses, circumcised on the eighth day, was conscious of being a Jew, and proud of his people and of his synagogue. He taught his disciples to serve it in all faithfulness and loyalty. The temple of Jerusalem was his temple, and he was jealous of its dignity and proud of its beauty. When Jesus saw the impending destruction of Jerusalem, the Capitol of his people, he cried tears of sorrow over it: "As he drew near and came in sight of the city," said Luke, "he shed tears, weeping over it and said: "A time is coming when your enemies will raise fortifications all around...They will dash you and the children inside your walls to the ground. Jerusalem, Jerusalem, how often have I longed to gather your child, as a hen gathers her brood under her wings..."" (Luke 19:41 and 13:34 sq.). What tenderness and what love for Jerusalem! Jerusalem was at the heart of Jesus as much as it still is today at the heart of any other zealous Jew.

Furthermore, Jesus lived the religious life of his people in all loyalty and faithfulness, going up to the holy City for all the celebrations of his nation and of his earthly family. For Jesus, his Jewish world was a reality of ordered harmony between man and God. Jewishness meant that everything from stones to angels, from society and politics to law, was ordered for man, for his happiness, for his well being and for his joy (See parables).

For Jesus, Jewishness meant also the plan of God for man to be free like God himself, to be all confident in his own nature and thus to attain to God. He knew also and taught that, unaided, man cannot alone rise to the height of God. He promised to send to his Jewish people and to the whole human race the Holy Spirit of God who will shake them out of their timeless slumber. Jesus has granted a sudden illumination to sightless eyes and enkindled new passions in cold souls. A new vision and fresh precisions had gushed from a Jewish heart and mind to quicken the universe.

CHAPTER 8

COVENANT WITH JESUS CHRIST

The basic truth that makes all the alliances of God real and true is the Incarnation.

The whole cloud of witnesses from Noah to Abraham, from Moses to the Prophets, the whole heroic survival of the people of Israel, point to this unique and marvelous happening. In fact, at the "fulfillment of time," at a crossroads in the history of creation, at a point in the march of mankind, the Second Person of the Trinity, the God of God and Creator of all, opened heaven to earth. He came down, dwelt in a womb, and he became Son of Man whose name was Jesus. The Invisible took a human form and was born from a woman. The Son of God assumed humanity, the very matter that surrounds and makes humanity. The Promised of the Father, he who was promised to Abraham, to Moses, to the Prophets and to all mankind, became a human reality, the Christ. This is the Incarnation.

THE INCARNATION

What a reality! God became man so that man can become God! Because the Son of God became man, man became his brother, and he became also Son of God by grace and dwelling place of the Holy Spirit.

In his Incarnation, the Son of God did not lose his divinity. Being God, he remained one with the Father. Being man, he became one with man and one with the matter that makes up man. In his Person, therefore, Jesus Christ unites the Creator with his creature and bridges the abyss that separates the Infinite and the finite. United in him, man and matter are sanctified, purified, and saved, and through him they are returned and united to their source and origin, the Father.

According to the biblical understanding, man is not, like in Greek philosophy, an incarnate soul. He is an animated body. In the Bible, the word "body" is a term that stands for man in essential unity with all men, and in solidarity with the created universe. Being a material body, man is one with the whole material creation. When the Son of God became man, he became one with every man and one with the whole created universe, as Adam was one with all mankind and with the material creation. The whole creation fell into sin when he fell into it.

In Jesus' understanding, which is the understanding of the Bible, the body is part of the matter of the universe; it is an element that unites the whole universe and makes it one. On the contrary, for Greek philosophy, matter is limitation, separation, consequently, harmful, unnecessary and to be spurned. For the Hebrew mind, the mind of Christ, of Saint Paul and of Christianity, it is rather an element of union, of unity and of complete solidarity. This is how God expressed his love for his creation, and revealed the fraternity that links all men to the fatherhood of God. He expressed this in the Incarnation of his Son.

St. Paul explains this unity between man and the universe in the Son of God by two biblical symbols or figures, one taken from harvest time, and the other from the creation of Adam.

At harvest time, the first sheaf of grain offered to God signifies that the entire land and all its produce belong to God. The consecration of the first part, or "first fruit," is really the consecration of the whole land. So, says St. Paul, Christ is the "first fruit" of humanity. Since Christ has been consecrated to God, since he is one with God, all humanity and all creation belongs entirely to God, and, in Christ, they are united to God. "Christ is the first born of a multitude of brothers." Everything and everyone is in Christ, in continual process of sharing in his life, death and resurrection. So, Christ is not only a Person: he is a community. In him, God, humankind, and material creation are epitomized and united.

Again and again St. Paul explains that Jesus is the New Adam, the first of a new humanity. As in the fall of the First Adam, all men and creation fell into sin, so in Christ the Second Adam, man and the whole creation have life and resurrection (Rom. 5:13-18). This is the solidarity expressed in the unity of one in all and all in one. This is the expression of God's love in the history of salvation.

When the Son of God became Son of Man he did not become a

doctrine or a fixed teaching. He became a real Man in a perfect human body. He was conceived in the womb. He developed, grew, died, rose and ascended in his human body to fill the whole universe with his eternal activity. This activity of the risen and ascended Lord radiates life and resurrection and encompasses the whole of creation from the Incarnation until the consummation of all times.

In the celebration of the Incarnation, the Christian first remembers what the answer of a girl of our human race has accomplished. The acceptance of the invitation of God brought down the Spirit of God who overshadowed Mary and fructified her womb with a divine seed, which, with her own seed, formed a human body. And it is this human body that the Son of God assumed; thus he became the Son of a girl of our race. He became our brother and co pilgrim in life. The Incarnation is a vision of wonder and bliss, a reality that lives in the now of every human life:

Today is The Promised Day!
God become man!
Today is the announcement of joy,
Today is the virginal festivity.
Today heaven is joined to earth.
Adam is renewed and Eve released from sorrow!
Our human body becomes the dwelling place
And the very temple of God.
Our humanity has been deified!
Wherefore, let us sing for joy! (661)

The human body now becomes the dwelling place of God, his temple, the place of his delight and the receptacle of the divinity. The Christian is thrilled by the realization of what has happened, and he announces it to every human ear that can hear it. The drama God is playing with humanity is a source of admiration and awesome adoration, a joyous celebration":

Listen, O heavens! And give ear, O ye earth!
The way of condescension is incomprehensible, And the manner of conception ineffable!
An angel announces the marvel.
A virgin's womb receives the Son of God,
The Holy Spirit is sent down to perform the miracle,
And the Father on high is well pleased...

Wherefore we sing to you with joy,
O God who were incarnate of her
And yet suffered no change in your divinity.
Bestow your peace and your mercy upon the world (661).

The Incarnation is the greatest drama that heaven and earth ever witnessed. Nothing can really convey its message except poetry, admiration and glorification. Indeed, the Christian Church enshrines it in a poetical setting, in music, and in hymns of exaltation strung together like pearls.

Since that moment of the Incarnation two thousand years ago, God is really, physically present in this world. He is living in this world. Since that moment of his Incarnation, God is working everywhere on earth. "Emmanuel" means that God is, "with us" and not only "in us." He walks with us. He lives and he suffers. He sings and he cries with the world in the person of the most glorious and in the most wretched of his people. He is "Emmanuel."

Yet, what is most astonishing and most marvelous in the Incarnation is that God has ceased to be, like for the Greeks, an abstract "totality," or "goodness," or "an immobile mover" of the universe. God took a human face and he became an object for our touch, ears, eyes, and smell, a real vibrant human being. God let himself be contained by matter, while in his divine reality he contains the whole universe. He did not swallow matter as a prey, but it became a part of his own prayerful attitude of thanks and glorification, bursting with divinity.

God is Light, and Christianity is the announcer of light, of beauty and of goodness. It is above all the religion of the Incarnation. Nietzsche accused it of being the "religion of the soul." He called it a "Platonism for the people." Christianity is rather the religion of beauty and harmony, of joy and hope. Its deepest intuitions still flow from its Hebrew origins and mentality.

The eyes of the Bible see and comprehend that flesh and spirit, matter and soul are wedded together. In his Incarnation, God the Son wedded the human body, and the human body became the humanity of God. The Resurrection does not dematerialize the body but makes it more "dense" and packed wit hall the matter of creation. The Resurrection and Ascension transfigure the body and creation, changing the world from a tomb and darkness and revealing it to be light, life and an object of thanks:

Behold, our divinization is now manifest,

for God is ineffably joined to mankind.

The old error has vanished
at the voice of the Archangel.

The Virgin has accepted the joyful news,
the earth has become heaven and the world
has been relieved of the original curse.

Let therefore the whole creation rejoice and
sing a hymn of praise:

O Lord, our Maker and Redeemer,
glory to You! (660).

THE APPEARANCE OF GOD IN THE FLESH: CHRISTMAS

The "Birth of the Invincible Sun," *Natalis Solis Invicti*, was a great
pagan feast. It was celebrated in Rome almost three hundred years
before the birth of Christ, at the time of the Emperor Aurelian Caesar
(274 A.D.). To replace this "pagan celebration," the Church of Rome
had the ingenious idea to claim that Christ was born on that day. Before
that date, the Christian world was celebrating Christ's birth in July, as
logic and history would dictate. The Eastern Church thought that the
idea of celebrating Christmas on the day of the "Invincible Sun" was
good, and adopted it. Christmas, on the 25th of December, is a purely
Christian invention. In Western as well as in Eastern Churches,
December 25th became the celebration of the real Sun, the Sun of
Justice, the Sun and Light of the world, "the light of Light, true God of
true God," Jesus Christ:

> Your Nativity, O Christ our God, has shed the Light upon the world.
> Through it we learned to worship You, O Sun of justice,
> And to recognize in You the only real Sun who Rises and who comes
> from on High.
> O Lord, glory to You (559).

The Son of God was conceived in the womb at the Incarnation. He
took on all the forms a human fetus experiences in a mother's womb.
And he was born. At the Incarnation, God became present in matter.

At his birth, he became visible to the human senses. The Unnamable acquires a name, Jesus, and the Untouchable becomes a suckling at the breast .God becomes the object of our amazed eyes and of our delighted touch, and a thrill to our five senses. At the Incarnation, God became human flesh, a seedling in the womb. At Christmas, he became visible. He opened the womb of his mother and came out of her to be visible and touchable. On that occasion, the Gospels tell us that angels sang and danced, not only in heaven but in the skies of our earth. Humble shepherds witnessed the astonishing miracle, and Magi came from the East to experience the happening.

So, at the birth of Christ, the skies exploded with joy and feasting. The universe stirred and offered the best star from its galaxies. The earth presented a cave. Animals presented their warm breath. Kings proffered their gold, frankincense and myrrh. The poor offered praise and admiration. Humanity gave a mother, a jewel of a mother, a mother more mother than any mother because she did not share her Son with a human father.

A Jewish girl from Galilee held in her arms the God of all. Like every baby born of a woman, when God came out of her womb and appeared in the flesh, he uttered the loud cry of existence: "Waaa! Here I am." This "I am" of existence, which God had only whispered once before, in the ear of Moses at Sinai, resounded now with vibrations throughout the universe. For the first time since creation began, the infinity of the galaxies registered the sound of their "master's voice." The devil heard it too and was thrilled by that voice that heals and saves.

Man shall never cease admiring, praising, singing for joy and happiness at the sight of God in the flesh. "Joy to the world!" Man can see now his face "and not die." The Eastern Church sings and praises with an awesome enthusiasm the sight of God "grazing" on the warm breasts of a woman of our race. And John the beloved disciple and theologian declares that the "glory of God" has been manifested in the delicate lines of a naked body. The glory of God was manifest in the flesh. Christmas was God's idea, and the manifestation of his concern and love.

The beauty of this memorial is beyond all beauty. The thrill and joy of God and of the whole universe is overflowing with generosity. And generosity becomes dizziness. Christians in particular want to imitate God And nature and overflow with generosity also. They wish to create happiness and joy and reproduce in others the joy which God is showering on them and on the whole universe. They shop and spend their savings and walk on tired feet to create joy. Christmas is filled with light and songs and the excitement of meetings. Christmas is a Christian celebration!

How sad it is to see some modern Christians combating this celebration, forgetting that festivities and exuberant demonstrations are integral parts of Christian mission, necessary to show how real is the revelation of the Living God. Our God is alive, always saving, always loving, pouring on us joy and happiness. Great campaigns, with apparently innocent slogans like "Let us put Christ back into Christmas!" will destroy the Feast. They really mean, "let us kill the joy of Christmas!" We have already killed too many meaningful Christian feasts. Without the exuberance, joy and enthusiasm, Christmas will also die, killed by our complexes of fear and pusillanimity. We have already killed the Ascension, the Assumption, the splendid feasts of the Incarnation, of the Trinity, and of the Transfiguration. Let us not kill Christmas too!

Christians of America owe a special debt of thanks to their brothers the Jews who through their Christmas parades keep alive the joy of the feast, while Saint Patrick parades are shrinking every year in number, joy and enthusiasm.

When the notes of Christmas music sound, there are no more pagan voices, there are no more pagan ears, no more indifferent hearts. God became visible to hear and sanctify hearing, to touch and sanctify human touch, to see with human eyes and sanctify all eyes, all colors and all parades. He cried like every baby born of a woman and thereby divinized every vibration of the universe. There is a third world of poverty and hunger and privation of doctors and nurses because we Christians have not taken God seriously and have not yet learned how to celebrate his birth.

We bless and magnify all those singers, carolers, and artists whose musical talents praise our new born God and Lord and Savior Jesus Christ.

This is the greatest aspect of the Alliance of God with Jesus Christ and through him with the whole world: the Incarnation made visible at the "Appearance of God in the flesh," Christmas.

THE HUMAN BODY

God the Father offered human flesh to his Son not because he hated him or wanted to punish him but because he loved him. The human flesh is therefore the greatest and most precious gift God can ever give besides himself. The Christian considers that the human body is the height of the expression of God's power and artistic ability. According to natural sciences, and the little they know and teach, since the time man became conscious of himself and of his surroundings, every function and every part of the body is an amazing miracle of composition, engineering, and functioning. World Olympics, beauty contests, colorful parades of people and sounds are essentially Christian. They are hymns to God's majesty and goodness, and they witness to the reality of the Incarnation.

The wonder of God's plan of creation is that he joined matter and spirit, not as a punishment, but as the expression of his love. The body is not a prison but a bride. Body and soul are wedded in love. Naturally the spirit rules, but its rule is a rule of love, not of tyranny, not of suppression or destruction. It is not just the spirit but the body also which holds God, physically and functionally.

One cannot be awake to God if he is not attuned to the powerful presence of his body. Even the physical postures of the body are a spiritual language God designed and made all the functions of the body, with its capacities and potentialities, out of love. Our spirit or soul cannot accept love, or respond to love, or search for beauty, truth and freedom except through the activities of the body. The power to accept God and enrich others the way God enriches us is conditioned by the attitude to one's own body, to one's personality, which is composed of body and soul.

Christ was formed by his people, Israel. He was born in a nation whose daily life was steeped in public prayers, and who always remembered the great deeds of God in public demonstrations. It is in such demonstrations that the Jews learned the proud passion of living. It was in public ceremonies that they announced to the world the uniqueness and goodness of God. Christ prayed with his people. It is in the assembly of the synagogue that he celebrated God and his people Israel.

The fluid mind of the Semite has no use for static concepts. Even in prayer, he takes ready refuge in physical images to express the unimaginable. His prayer to God is in his body which sways rhythmically. He raises and lowers his eyes. He mumbles and mutters and sighs loud and clear. In prayer, he voices acceptance with sounds of joy, or reproves a deed with eloquent indignation. Sometimes he stops his prayer to exchange a feeling, an inspiration, or a hope.

But his seriousness of purpose becomes light and strength, filled with an invisible beauty. His joy is expressed in chanting, dancing, making melodies that no other melody can equal. God is seen as present among his people. The "Shekina," the glory of God, becomes visible and the impossible becomes real. This was the regular prayer of Jesus, his daily celebration of God. This was the very same daily atmosphere Christians lived in for centuries. This is the atmosphere that still animates Christian assemblies.

The whole marvelous organism that man is speaks of God. All his energies are the expression of an infinite love. He reverences and honors them. Man does not offer what he has but what he is. Strictly speaking, he does not have moments of adoration and praise: All his life, every act, every gesture, the smile in his face, is, or becomes, a song of adoration and of offering, a prayer. Man's faculties, all of man's energies and passions, are meant to be instruments with which to bless God. When the senses of man, therefore, enter into discovery or enjoyment, they enter into relation with God. Shunning any earthly beauty, sound, color, good performance, or any blessing of this body is an offense to the fate of God. Every human endeavor is a hymn of joy and praise and should be transformed into a message of goodness.

A stilted attitude in the presence of life is the sign of a cold and boring religion. Dance, singing, and movement are expressions of life and of being alive.

Man, and especially the Christian, cannot be oblivious of his body when he wants to enter into communion with God. Action and motion determine and define him because action and movement necessitate choice and commitment. The Christian sings his song. The New Testament integrates the fresh outlook of enthusiasm of the children of the Gospel with the earthy, existential and experiential mentality of the Old Testament into a beautiful hymn of movement made in the flesh.

The body is the sign and symbol, the sum of all the powers and forces that make divinity present. Bowing again and again, sighing a word, offering clouds of perfumed incense rising to heaven, these witness to the unity of the human person and awaken him to God. Body and soul move in unison, and man is able to listen to God and to reveal himself. He prays. Prayer is communication, communion with others and with God. Jesus the Lord exhaled upon his Apostles to signify by his breath the coming of the "breath of God," "the Holy Spirit." The priest "breathes upon the water and upon the face of the one to be baptized" to signify also the coming of this same Spirit of God who is thus communicated by the breath and gesture of the body. He makes with his hand signs and gestures to impart by them the grace of God and his healing presence.

Our modern Christianity has been infected with some philosophical currents of thought which teach that the body has to be banished and punished as a hindrance to our communication with God. Stoicism, Platonism, Neo-Platonism, dualism, and later on, in history, Jansenism, thought the body was a scary shadow and a heavy weight that shackled the soul in her flight to the higher spheres of contemplation. It was a prison to be destroyed. Platonism claimed that from a "Supreme Being of the universe" up there "somewhere" emanates the human soul which is cast down into this miserable world and imprisoned in this wretched body.

Christian Churches have been more or less infected by this doctrine which urges man to run forever to the desert. Man has to punish the body and beat it and deprive it of as many necessities as one can, in order to keep it in slavery until it frees the soul. Only when the soul is free and escapes from matter can it return to the place where it came from.

To this Platonism that prevailed in the Christian Churches for a long time was added the stress on moralism. Restraint from bodily movement and from outward expression of joy castrated Christian celebration and killed its witness. Thus the divine events of the Incarnation, of the Ascension, of Transfiguration, of the Trinity of God, and of the Assumption of the Mother of God, have been emptied of their meaningful beauty and of their message of hope, joy, and glory. Our pretentious intellectualism and lack of enthusiasm in the spirit have killed these celebrations which otherwise are laden with announcements of good news and of joy. In the practical life of the Church they are dead! Easter would die too were it not for the new hat and the new dress and the flowers and perfumes of the season!

The genuine Christian language is completely different from that of Plato and of Greek philosophy in general. Christianity teaches that when the Word of God became flesh "We beheld his glory" (John 1:14), which means his beauty, and his grandeur. In the fragile and delicate lines of the naked body we see all we need to know about God. "He who sees me, sees the Father." It is by learning Jesus Christ that we learn God. Learning Jesus is to embrace his flesh, hear his human voice, and eat his Body and drink his Blood. It is in and through the bodily encounter with the Sacraments that God is imparted to us.

Sanctifying grace is not a thing different from God but God himself in his uncreated energy who comes to dwell in us, in our body and soul, in every part of us, and not only somewhere "in the soul." When the sacraments are applied to the human body, this body becomes the meeting point where the mutual relation and personal union of grace comes to fruition. It is in this bodily embrace that the union of God and man is realized and intensified. It is in his bodily presence and reality that man meets and receives Christ. It is in the matter of the sacrament and in the body of man that Christ is present to man and man to God. The reality of grace is indeed this mutual personal presence of Christ and man, embodied and expressed in the sacrament.

Not only pagan philosophies influenced Christians to shun much participation of the body in their worship. There is also the natural tendency of man to build zones and fences around himself to protect his autonomy, independence and privacy. Man has the tendency to isolate himself from others. But Jesus, on the contrary, urges the Christian to invade and be invaded, to open himself to his own consciousness and to others.

Jesus himself invaded space and human boundaries. He invaded the privacy of many men and women and threw them right into the midst of crowds. He invaded Peter and washed his feet .He told his followers to serve and to teach, which are forms of invading the space and defenses of others. Man cannot achieve emotional freedom in many cases unless he reaches beyond his personal space, breaks through the masks he sets up and self protection, and touches other people and conveys to them his presence.

Jesus showed also that celebration and prayer are thrusts forward towards the shores of God. They are movements of the whole person, opening and revealing. He was never scared of storms and darkness from which one hides or runs away. Many times he had to reassure his followers and inspire them with courage to face what they considered a menace. He walked on stormy seas and calmed them when he had neither sails nor oars. Christ recreated constantly and without hesitation openness to others. He constantly recreated love, freedom, admiration and joy in the solitude of the desert, as well as in the big cities of Samaria and Jerusalem. It was in his bodily gesture and words and touch that he communicated his Father. He sent the Holy Spirit to dwell on the heads of the Apostles and not in their souls. He sent him as a Wind and as a fiery Flame.

Christ urges also to be "awake," to be attentive and always on the "look out" for his coming in the body. He is the "Bridegroom" who comes to seek his Bride. Only those who are awake and alive can enter the Kingdom.

The presence of beauty and the sense of beauty are conditions for being awake. The experience of beauty is the most favorable atmosphere for wakefulness. The place of prayer must be therefore a place aglow with beauty and beautiful things in order to make man feel that he is in contact with another world. Beautiful Churches and expensive things displayed in Christian churches are not "for the glory of God." God does not need temples, churches, expensive or not expensive displays of colors, perfumes and artistic forms. Man needs all this. They are done or made for the joy and glory of man.

People in prayer should see the saints around them, wrapped in their icons with a mantle of eternity; candles flickering in a thousand hues of light; incense whirling in a warm atmosphere; music swelling from every corner of the assembled congregation; vestments of multicolors and designs which sway and shine. The deacons move around between the people and the celebrant. In the middle of the sanctuary stands the Bishop, image of Christ, presiding over the celebration. Every act, gesture and movement of the body has its meaning. Every person performing a bodily gesture in the celebration points to a spiritual reality and acclaims it.

Our human body is the sign of the great love of the Artist, God. It has to sing and sway and be open in all directions, even to pain and death. God will fill it with his love. This is one of the aspects of the Incarnation of God where he became Man so that man becomes by grace, God!

CHAPTER 9

THE POEM OF JESUS CHRIST

In all the reality of his person and of his mission, Jesus the Christ was a Jew sent by God to Jews only. In fact, he spent all his life, and exercised his whole mission exclusively in his Jewish surroundings and among his own Jewish people. "I have been sent," said he, "only to the lost sheep of the people of Israel" (Matt. 15,24). If he made a couple of forays into Samaritan or Phoenician lands, it was only a passing through, and a stop between points through his own land of Israel.

The essential point of the mission of Jesus was to call his people, the Jews, to liberty and freedom as much as it was to call them to holiness. It was to call the absolute primacy of the person beyond social convention, beyond the primacy of law and human tradition. Christ calls all humanity to freedom, to a new kind of life and service, specifically that of love. Being subject to laws that are impossible to satisfy in their entirety is a slavery. This does not mean that the Law or laws in themselves are bad, but that man in his native, existential condition has not the power to fulfill them, or, the least we can say, that he cannot fulfill them without assistance. Alone he is impotent, he cannot measure up to them. His state of impotence slides into a state of self resentment, of guilt, and consequently, of slavery and sin. When man belongs to other than himself he is a slave and a sinner.

Jesus' mission was to free, not only his Jewish people but through them, all peoples, and lead all mankind to the freedom of the children of God, which is the freedom to love. Poured forth from God, love participates in the freedom of God because it seeks the interest of God which is primarily the good of the community. To love is therefore to be free.

At the time of Christ the daily prescriptions of the Jewish Law were so innumerable and so complicated that they were almost impossible to follow, especially for the common people. There was the Law of Moses. There were the pronouncements of the Prophets. There were also, to quote a great Jewish writer: "The Communities' memory of Judges' decisions and ancestors' practices, a written mass of rules, ordinances and cases law codes and digests which had grown year by year…laws with their many facets of interpretations of interpretations. A complete edition of these laws would comprise today thirty-five tomes, each about a foot and a half tall, half foot thick, two solid type columns…" According to any standard of human thought, these laws would be "a sealed book unless one spends a whole life long, starts at a real tender age and grows old in their thirty-five thick English translated volumes." Furthermore, "It would be a gigantic miracle for the human brain to hold all the details of these laws and come out of them with sanity and some kind of human joy and smile…" (Herman Wouk). Only a very few great Jewish saints did it.

At the time of Christ, the prescriptions that a religious Jew had to observe in his daily life were 613 in number. There were 248 positive and 365 negative prescriptions. These prescriptions were the guides to conduct and considered to be a secure means of winning divine favor and salvation. Besides, they were all of the same binding forces because they were thought to spring from God's inspiration and will. The most minute ones were just as binding as the most serious. The rabbinic teaching was: "Anyone who eats bread without washing first his hands will incur the same condemnation as the one who frequents a prostitute." Another rabbinic tradition pushed the glorification of these laws to such an extent that "God himself" was said to "study the laws every day and that He was their first practitioner." The study of the law was therefore a daily necessity for every good Jew.

The common people who did not know all the prescriptions of the Law were judged to be transgressors of the Law, impure, and therefore to be avoided. "They were accursed!" These legal impurities were incurred not only by transgressors but also by anyone who came in contact with these transgressors. The word "Pharisee" means precisely that, "separate" from the common mass of the people and "aloof" from the crowd.

These Pharisees were against Jesus, because Jesus was always mixing with the common people, the ignorant and "sinners." To the Pharisees he was a sinner. But the common people looked up to him as a teacher and a rabbi. He claimed that he was "from God," and people believed him to be so. The Scribes and the Pharisees thought that if he was what he pretended to be, he should be rather a mirror of the Law. He should be a faithful practitioner of the prescriptions in all their details and rigor. They thought and taught that these prescriptions were from God; therefore, they had to be followed in their integrity. It was only by following these rules that man could placate the irate God and attain to salvation.

On the contrary, Jesus stated clearly that the righteousness coming from practicing these prescriptions of the Law was not sufficient: "I say to you, that unless your righteousness surpasses that of the Scribes and the Pharisees, you shall not enter the Kingdom of heaven" (Mt. 5:20). The mission of Jesus Christ among his people was also to give his people the power of freedom, a power that comes from within, allowing them to do all and more than is required by Law. Man thirsts for freedom, for a life without external coercion; but above all he thirsts for that internal freedom in which the forces of love, intelligence and life can flower and bloom. This is possible only by the power of personal freedom which is of God, and from the special action of the Holy Spirit of God whom Christ was to send to his followers. Thus freed and strengthened, man can fulfill not only the Law but he can do so joyously, freely and spontaneously. "The Lord is Spirit, and where the spirit of the Lord is there is freedom" (II Cor. 3:17).

Historically speaking, the early Christians were zealous observers of the Law of Moses. St. Paul, the great Jewish leader, approved of Jewish Christians who remained faithful to their ancestral laws (1 Cor. 9:20; Acts 16:3; 21:26). But the more Paul studied the message of Christ and understood the fullness of its meaning, the more he himself and the first Jewish Christians with him realized that the coming of Christ freed them from the prescriptions of the Law. Christ was really the "end of the law" (Rom. 10:14). One could be saved through faith in him who had died and was risen (Gal. 5:4; 2:4; 4:1-7).

On the other hand, and practically speaking, Jesus, like his own Jewish people, regarded Yahweh's law and demands as completely reasonable and acceptable. He said it plainly: "Do not think that I came to abolish the law and the prophets but to fulfill them. For truly I say to you, until heaven and earth pass away not the smallest letter or stroke of the Law shall pass away" (Matt. 5:17). Therefore, Christ did not abolish the Law. He rather gave it a new dimension, a new interpretation. For him old truths do not disappear. They are absorbed. Applied to a new era of salvation, they acquire a new meaning.

The Holy Spirit of God that Jesus promised to send was the One who transforms not only the meaning of the Law but the attitude of man toward the law. He was to empower man to fulfill the law in all its integrity and bring about the "Kingdom of God." This Spirit teaches truths which attract, which inflame the heart, which give birth to hope, and which inspire men to vital and dynamic action. Christian freedom is to be absorbed into the truth of Christ. He to whom Christ reveals his face is in the truth and sees the face of God. "The truth will make you free" (John 8:32). The Kingdom of God for Jesus was not brought about by fulfilling a specific law or laws but by bringing man himself, the whole of man, to the fullness of freedom and joy. When God can freely flow in man like a river of living water and fill him with his own life, there is freedom and joy. Law or laws are then a ladder that man uses to open himself to God and to ascend to God in order to be filled by him. They are not an obligation that enslaves him by guilt.

The Sabbath, for instance, was a sacred to Jesus as it was to any good religious Jew of his time. The Sabbath was a feast made up of light and peace and joy, a feast of delight and trust because "God blessed it and made it holy." "He rested on the Sabbath from all the work he had done in creation" (Gen. 2:3). No one can undo or abolish that which God has ordered. For Christ, the Sabbath was a day of ennobling pleasure made of free man and heal him from all miseries. So Christ loved and honored the Sabbath.

Throughout the pages of the Gospels we see Jesus going faithfully into the synagogue on the Sabbath to preach and teach the Torah, the Word of God. If Christ did anything to the Sabbath he made it more ennobling by overruling its rigidity and unbending taboos that enslaved man. "The Sabbath was made for man," he declared, "not man for the Sabbath" (Mk. 2:23; 3:5). It is like the State, the Church, order, money, revolution, science, morality, sexuality and beauty. These are made for man and not man for them. He who listens to this voice of Christ becomes free in regard to everything. He is not a slave to anything any more. He does not bow to idols and bind himself to them. Only God is absolute and the Absolute does not rape, he does not force. He is not even a burden. He makes us free.

So now we can proclaim the real meaning of the message of Christ. Christ wants his Jewish people, and through them the whole world, to turn from laws to persons, from obligation to a loving response, from self to others, from duty to grace, and from work to faith. This was the new vision of the Gospel. This was the moral revolution of Christ.

There is no real revolution without love. Christ believed that after thousands of years bound to God by laws, man had come to maturity. Jesus refused to believe that man should be shackled forever by a fixed form. Man and the world have a tremendous power of creativity. Man no longer should feel dominated by nature or obliged to serve blindly human traditions. On the contrary, he should feel he is the master or at least a partner of nature and of the world, and that there are no more limitations to his dignity. Christ had confidence in the union of man with creation, and he thought that in this meeting of man and nature, man and all members of society could attain to God. He did not bind man to old forms. Rather he preached and practiced a radicalism full of courage and audacity, leading beyond the limits of this world, not downward but upward.

The life of Jesus was entirely made up of what is rare to find in man: personal decisions. Man is easily stifled by the chains of habit. He needs the magic of the new and the unknown. So Jesus wanted the life of his Jewish people, the life of man, to be likewise free and filled with an ever new strength for decision a new dream, an Apocalypse, which means revelation. He refused the security of the law as the only means to attain to God. He wanted the life of man to be a life of imagination, invention and risk. These inner thirsts incite man to continually change and progress and experiment, not counting the costs in efforts and self-denial. And if there is a fall, even the fall will attain to the triumph of resurrection and to the fullness of joy.

Jesus was a real and sincere Jew. He did not despise the Law of Moses or the Prophets wherein his people the Jews tried to find security and salvation. He rather wanted them to go on respecting and practicing them but at the same time taking risks and being forever like the beginning of the universe free, forever free. Moral and religious traditions should lead to interior freedom. But Christ saw that moral and religious traditions created the chains of egotistic instincts, social conventions and of unjust authority. They had rather stifled personal decision and personal freedom instead of giving birth to them. Christ rejected their rigidity and the blind force of their obligation.

A poem is a mockery to logic because a poem expresses God's freedom and beauty. Christ wanted man's life to be a poem. He himself was a poet and his life was a great poem. Never does he act through routine or revolt, but always with new ingenuity which thrills with surprises. If prayer is a listening, faith is acceptable of a surprise: "Unless you become like little children you shall not enter the kingdom of heaven." Christ tried to "poetize" human life by symbols, gestures, by his parables, by sounds, by his stories about workers and salaries, about weddings and big banquets, about birds, flowers, vineyards and wine. Being thus a poem and a never ending source of surprise, man's life will have real meaning.

This is the message of Christ to the world, a message inspired by a Jewish soul and sung in a Jewish culture and mentality.

Besides this new vision of freedom, the most stunning and most exhilarating reality that Christ the Jew brought to the world Resurrection. Resurrection is not a new life, but life itself transfigured and transformed. The old seed of life dies, and in the very process of dying it is given birth. Life rejoices in death, because death acquires a new meaning: it has a new outlook, a new impetus to bring about fullness of life.

Christ had suffered an died on the cross at the hand of the powerful Romans. He was buried or three days. On the third day Yahweh raised him from the grace. This is Resurrection. Resurrection shows the real meaning of death which springs into life, into light, into joy and into security unmatched and unending. Risen and truly alive, Jesus appeared to his Jewish disciples, to his Jewish contemporaries, and to his friends over a period of forty days. In all his apparitions he was in the fullness of joy because he was completely possessed by God, completely free. The people to whom he appeared were all Jews, in a Jewish land, and belonged to a Jewish way of life. He wanted to be possessed by God and to be free.

The fact of the Resurrection was not a Roman idea. Neither was it in any way of Greek inspiration. It was, rather, a complete contradiction to what Greek and Roman philosophies stood for. Jews, and only pure-blooded Jews, stressed it, explained it and proved it. These Jews did not tire of saying: "What we have seen with our eyes, what we have touched with our hands, what we have heard with our ears, that is what we are preaching to you" (1 Jn. 1:1). Only Jews, disciples of freedom, could and did witness to it.

And the world, bewildered and scandalized, believed and became free. The world believed the amazing beauty and radiance coming out of such a reality, the Resurrection, the New Passover from slavery to freedom and from death to life. The Jews were witnessing to a fellow

Jew, preaching and proclaiming his Resurrection was a hymn of exaltation sung to the glory of God in his faithfulness to his Covenant. Christian faith, Christian life and love, all came out of a Jewish song, out of a Jewish womb.

Legend for Jews and reality for Christians, the conviction of the Resurrection of Jesus Christ, and consequently of the real freedom man is called to live by, came out of the experience of the Jewish people and from the substance of their very being. Legend for Jews and reality for Christians, such a sublime preaching cannot come but from a people whose reality is above any human reality, pointing and witnessing to the Beyond and to the Only One who can give a meaning to life and to death. If there is a glory and a triumph in Christian life, it should be remembered with thanks to such a people, the Jewish people of Jesus Christ.

To the eyes of the angels, to the eyes of the human heart, Christ, the Savior of mankind, is an ever living and ever present reality. He is invisible and yet always here. He has died and yet he is alive. He has gone and yet he is always coming, always present. Forever alive! Forever free! For me, a Christian, as for all Christians, the Jewish people are still witnesses to the memory of the unbelievable beauty of Jesus Christ, the Son of David, Son of Israel, Son of Abraham, Son of Adam, Son of God. He is the unfolding and only answer to the mystery that shines out of their very name…Israel.

Man is always reaching out, always searching for completeness and totality. When man meets the risen Christ he bursts into freedom, and into hymns of praise and glory. He has to attain to that part of life that cannot be seen or measured, to that freedom which is the glory of God in man; in Christ he can see it in its fullness. Without this view on freedom life is a problem, love is a problem, birth and death are problems. And living together becomes the greatest problem of all. For Christianity, the problem has been solved. Life, love, birth and death have become in Christ a beauty, a joy, a heaven and a beatitude. Thus freedom will link all humanity in the love that was poured by God into our hearts.

In this very same Christ, Judaism and Christianity burst upon the Jews and the Gentiles alike, and burst within them as well. They split and break the limits of all men wide open to bring them felicity, joy, life and freedom. With the risen Christ there is no more fear, no more death: "Where is your power, O death? Where is your sting, O Hades?" Thus the fact of the Resurrection of Christ makes every human face beautiful beyond description, the face of the Jew as well as of the

Christian, of the believer and non believer alike. The human face becomes a celebration and a feast. Every created thing, created by God or man made, is a priceless jewel reflecting the meaning of the Resurrection. This is a celebration. Hatred or division are banished because they destroy the face of the risen Lord like armed conflicts destroy the jewels of creation. In Christ, man's life becomes ever freer, ever larger and more meaningful, a celebration.

One cannot understand who Jesus Christ is, unless he is a poet inspired by God and a mystic. One cannot understand the meaning and the message of the Gospel unless he is full of the reality of being. Jesus Christ is more than a Savior, that is, more than what can be measured and weighed and analyzed by the physical eye. Christ is a giver. He is a Lover. Giver and Lover who gives and creates freedom, resurrection, salvation and redemption for all mankind. To understand the thrill that radiates from such a Savior, one has to have the eyes of angels, the eyes of God. He who celebrates has them in abundance.

CHAPTER 10

THE GOOD NEWS OF JESUS CHRIST

According to what we can gather from the life and teaching of Jesus Christ, the truth which is not mixed with one's own blood, truth which does not flow harmoniously into a beautiful gesture, or into a tender look, is poison. A spiritual message which does not carry first and foremost a shock, a poem, something from the heart, a communication of life, is a message betrayed; it is condemned to remain sterile. Every truth uttered by Jesus Christ is a truth that conveys life and joy because it has been first warmed in the heat of love.

The whole life of Christ, all his teaching, even his smallest gestures, are aimed at saving man from tyrannies and changing the water of this life into the wine of the Feast. The Gospel is the Charter of this freedom and dignity. The words of Christ, taken one by one or collectively, are a stirring experience of life, allowing man to go into life and live it fully. Christ's voice reaches an ecstasy beyond and above any voice ever heard on earth. The tone of his voice is a bearer of that sublime message that we are on our way to another lovelier world, tinted with unimaginable wonders, alive with ultimate music and bursting with radiance and joy. We are going to a "banquet," a "wedding," and a "kingdom." Only those who go beyond appearances, and contact the reality of persons and of things, are allowed into that Kingdom. God, man, creation, Christ and his entire life are so many reasons and subjects for wonder and joy that enable us to enter into that Kingdom. Each one is a poem and a miracle of beauty that makes us sing in glory, awe and joy. Each is a celebration designed to make our life a celebration.

THE GOSPEL OF JESUS CHRIST

The story of the life and of the deeds of Christ is called "Gospel," good news, because it is precisely news of life. The message of the Gospel penetrates to the heart and sweeps away sin and ugliness. It is always new because it is fraught with wonder. We Christians do not read; we proclaim the Gospel. Those who are gifted musicians and singers chant its words, its texts and its message. The Ancients always insisted, with a profound sense of wisdom, on the way the voice should be modulated, the way the words of the Gospel should be brought out. Whether elaborate or simple, the proclamation of the Gospel has this one function: To convey the poetry of the text and the feeling of glory and joy of being in the presence of God.

Simple proclamation differs but little from the spoken word. It is characterized by a pleasant tone of the voice, a gentle inflection, and a clear rendering of the meaning of the Word. The proclamation of the Gospel is an act of faith where we meet God in Jesus Christ.

We believe that the Gospel is light and the announcer of life. It is Christ communicating his Father; it is Christ himself communicated to the world in sound. Christ brings to the ear that listens and to the eye that reads the Spirit of God. Our blood carries its sound like pure oxygen to every joint and to every corner of our body, to inundate it with life, light and tenderness of heart.

Easterners call the Gospel the second Incarnation. Whereas in the first, the "Son of God" became "Son of man," in the second Incarnation, in the Gospel, the "Word of God" became "word of man," he became a Book. For this reason, the Gospel Book is always bound in silver, or gold or precious materials. He is always on our altars, as it were "God on his throne." The Gospel is carried in procession, borne aloft on our heads, incensed and kissed with reverence and devotion. St. John Chrysostom says: "When emperors of this world speak we all shout with one voice and one heart: 'Glory be to you, lord.' But when the Lord Jesus speaks in his Gospel our enthusiasm grows stronger and louder and we repeat it twice,: 'Glory be to You, O Lord Glory be to You.'" Our enthusiasm becomes love, and we repeat the cry twice, once before the proclamation of the Gospel, and once when the proclamation has ended.

One predominant idea of the Gospel's message is that we are safe in God. Christ did and said things that often appear to be impossible in order to bring us into the realization that we are not slaves. We are the children of God. When we enter into a relation with God, our relation is with a father. "Religion" is needed where there is a wall of separation between God and man. But Christ, who is both God and man, has broken down the wall between man and God. He has inaugurated a new life, a new relation between man and God. He has created and established a new life, not a new religion.

Because the Gospel is an invitation, not an exacting obligation, it flourishes and lives supreme in communities and in innumerable individuals. The Gospel is the power of God who inspires and shakes the lives of untold numbers of peoples. It is a ferment that will never go dry. "He started teaching them for a long time," says St. Matthew. He has not finished his instructions yet. The people of his town wanted to make him a King, to set him high and above the crowds and far away from the turmoil of life. But Jesus refused. He wanted to stay at his teaching job, in contact with everyone. The Christian God is not a "topic" that can be fixed in words and passed on to pupils. He is Life, whom Jesus calls with an amazing simplicity, Father.

In the celebration of the Gospel, Christ is continually multiplying life and spreading indefinitely its "contagion." Jesus is constantly pulling down the walls of our prison to set us free, and allowing us to celebrate God and life. In the presence of violence he proclaimed: "Blessed the peacemakers." To the indifferent, he talked of "violence." In response to the asceticism of the Pharisees and the Essenes, he drank and ate and went around with public sinners. He protested the economic privileges of priests by turning their tables over with a hard and violent whipping. With Herod he was silent! To Pilate he recalled that authority comes from on high! To all he left the invitation to love. "Love the enemies." "Love the pagans." "Love the Roman colonizers who were going to crucify him." He goes about creating life and freedom, the real inner freedom which brings man to God who is the Supreme Freedom, a Celebration of life: "Love as I have loved!"

The word Christ used in the Gospel as referring to God is bold, much bolder than any human intelligence can dare say. For Jesus Christ, God is more than a Father. He is an "Abba," a "Daddy," "A dearly beloved Father." Abba is a face, not a name, a face that shines, smiles, talks, plays and melts into the tenderness of love. Abba is light and life giving. By commanding us to call God "Abba," "Dad," Christ teaches that we are in relation with Forgiveness, Joy and ever present and ready

Salvation. That is what the word really mans in the mouth of Christ.

Such a relation with God makes us sing our life. We recognize our dignity to be really above heaven and earth, to be more value than all the miracles of the universe. This is an all important element of the Gospel of Christ. Our value is the highest and most sublime of all creation. We are the product of a love that is beyond all expression of love, the love of God who is a "Dad"! The "Wisdom" of God seems to be "A delighting game ever at play…, at play everywhere in the world, delighting to be with the sons of men" (Prov. 8:30). "God only unites with gods," says Symeon the New Theologian. And Gregory of Nazianzus gasps with delight: "Indeed, indeed man is a game in the heart of God."

THE "ABBA," FATHER

The word "Father," on the lips of those who believe in the message of Christ, adds power and dignity and heightens their already sublime role in creation. The early Church found the "Our Father" a devastating and frightening prayer. No one can utter such words unless he has overcome all inner unrest, all selfishness and all provincialism. At one point of history, the words of the "Our Father" were not revealed to neophytes until they were ready to be baptized and receive the Body and Blood of Holy Communion.

We are commended to say to this "Abba," "Thy kingdom come!" which means "take over," "be the only one who inspires, directs and rules my life." We say it with mixed emotions, but with daring. "Kingdom of God" means justice, peace and love. It is not simply a personal salvation and fulfillment, but it establishes a new order of things. Those in the kingdom give to whomever asks, treats all men as real children of God, forgives without question, resists evil.

The kingdom is characterized therefore by healing, forgiveness, sharing, reconciliation, all of which are acts a "family" shares and enjoys. God is a Father, Abba. The person who says the "Our Father" comprehends that he or she is united with everyone, and that all are equal in the eyes of God in whom they all find peace and salvation. They all belong to the kingdom: They are brothers and sisters. Whoever says the "Our Father" must say it aloud, because it is "Our." "Our" is the word of the community. Every member of the community must hear it. We say it also with arms open to the heavens, "Shamaim" to "the everywhere." It is in the "everywhere" indeed, that the "Abba" resides and dwells.

Abba is the One who makes happy and blessed those attacked and burdened by guilt or despair. He is with them everywhere. He is the "Dad" who can quiet all their inner discord, overcome their ills, and destroy their sense of guilt. Since he is "Dad," God makes them rather burst into praise, thanksgiving and song. He himself organizes for his children the greatest picnic ever, as he did for his prodigal son. Abba is love. A celebration! Infidelities and sins are wiped out and forgotten and forgiven.

"Hallowed be thy name" emphasizes the goodness of God in spite of our infidelities. God makes his name holy when he acts to save, thus making good his promises.

To illustrate this unbelievable truth that God "hallows his name," Christ told a bold story. One day, said he, a youngest son just out of college, full of starry eyed ideas and drunk with the power of his youth, approached his "Dad" with an incredible demand: He asked for his inheritance. Now an inheritance is only given once, after the parent has died and is buried. Wealth is security, strength and power one does not relinquish easily. One does not expose himself to need or dependence on others. No parent in his right mind, and certainly not an Oriental Father, were he the most dedicated and loving of all fathers, would sell business, house and everything accumulated through the years, and give it to a foolish youngster. Only a lover would weaken and accept defeat and surrender to foolishness. Christ said that God does surrender to such foolishness, because he is a special "Abba," a Lover.

The Son went away with all the riches of his "Dad." He looked for his happiness, for his real self. He searched in drugs. He searched in sex, in parties and orgies, and even in slavery. And "his self," his relation to life and love, was not there.

"Where is Abba?" said he. "Let's go home!" "Return home!" Metanoia!

Returning home is joy, dance, freedom and happiness. "Dad" had prepared a picnic for his son. Metanoia, going back home, repentance, is a celebration.

No difficulty or hardship has power over Christ. The Fathers of the Church stress very strongly that Christ wanted to "re create," "re vivify" what was interrupted by the fall of man. The healing of diseases was a figure. The healing of all sinners who opened themselves to that "physician of body and soul" was also a figure. They presented themselves and were accepted for what they were, sinners. In him, they became pure and holy. They accepted him for what he was, God, and they were deified.

Healing is also resurrection. The healing from death is a rather frequent happening in the Gospel. Healing and reconciliation are the golden thread that runs through the whole work of Christ. It is a return to the original bliss, to Paradise where God never ceases to reside. Going back home! Going back to the image of God.

THE BROTHER

If God is "Our Father," the "other" is a brother, my brother, the brother of Jesus Christ. "Whatever you have done even to the littlest one, you have done it to me," said Jesus. He put men into a terrible dilemma. Relations with others and hard, painful. They are a crucifixion. Sartre was not wrong when he declared that "hell is the other!" Christ knew that psychological situation better than Sartre and better than all psychoanalysts of all times. Relation with the "other" took him to Gethsemane, to Caiaphas, to Herod, and to the terrible crucifixion of the Romans. Yet he talked more often of forgiveness than of love.

Only forgiveness and reconciliation can make human relations possible. There is no love on earth, no friendship, no possible peace without forgiveness. In his "Our Father" Christ makes forgiveness an essential element of our relation with God. "Forgive us as we forgive the other." God freely offers forgiveness out of his gracious love. If we accept his forgiveness, our lives become one with him and we act out of the same frame of mind. We forgive, not because there is apology or sorrow or a good resolution on the part of the offender, but because of the goodness of God that fills us. "In that way you will become children of your Father in heaven" (Matt. 5:45). "Freely you have received. Freely give," said the Lord again.

Christ proclaimed forgiveness and reconciliation as the new way of living. We forgive only because we have received God's new life. Our relation with the "other" is the gamble of our life. We are afraid to be rejected, misunderstood, betrayed. So we hid in self centeredness which appears to be comfort and security. Christ came to teach us that the real meaning of hiding is loneliness and teach us that the real meaning of hiding is loneliness and suicide. It is the power of evil. It is evil. "Deliver us from the power of evil," "deliver us from evil." This is the paradox of the Word of the Lord Jesus: "When one loses himself (appearance), then he finds himself (reality)."

A man who refuses forgiveness or reconciliation to his brother is a prisoner of his solitude. He is lonely and hungry. A prisoner of his solitude. He is lonely and hungry. A prisoner is hungry for freedom, for light, for the real joy of life. Christ wants us to be free, to be "delivered from evil," from self centeredness, and egotism. He wants us to be open to our brother and the brother to us. Old Christian abbots, leaders of holy monks, did not exaggerate when they constantly reminded their monks to measure their closeness to God by their generosity in forgiving. Their saying went like this: "Do not talk about how long and how often you have prayed, fasted and abstained. If you forgive, you are monks. Only if you forgive from all your heart, and always, can you say: We are disciples of Christ."

The monks of a community of brothers in Caesarea of Palestine were full of the thought that by reason of their constant recitation of the psalms they were surpassing others in virtue. They received this admonition from their spiritual father:

Do not tell me how often you fast and abstain, how many times you repeat the prayer and sing the psalms. There is something greater. There is the command of the Gospel of our Lord Jesus Christ. Is there any among you, even the most advanced, who can understand the tired mankind of our day, who can command those who suffer? Is there anyone who can free those who have fallen into the snares of sin? Is there any one who can give peace to men? Who can enable them to come to love life, to rejoice and be thankful? The one who can really forgive and lead others to forgive is the real disciple of Christ! These acts of mercy will show that you really have made spiritual progress.

Voluntary death for the sake of the other is yet a greater love than love itself. Christ's death was the gift of himself to everyone, to the ones who believed in him as well as to the ones who betrayed him, to the ones who cursed him and renounced him, and to the one who sold him. God is that Source which is inaccessible and yet so intimately near because he is always forgiving. When we cross the frontiers of our individuality and extend our hearts to "the other," we are nearest to God. The Christian religion is not God's support for and approval of our weaknesses, or simply consolation in our day to ay pains and sorrows. It is rather a terrible judgment. Only if we accept this judgment can we look forward to the promise of the new life.

There is nothing more touching than the answer of Christ to the inquiry of the disciples of John the Baptist about the meaning of his mission. " 'Go tell, John,' he said, 'about what is happening in your very eyes: The blind receives his sight, the lame walk, the lepers are cleansed, the deaf hear, the dead are raised, and the poor have the good news preached to them'" (Matt. 11:1-5).

What a vista! The Abba is at work among his children! Misery is banished, sin vanquished, and the doom and gloom of the wrath of the old God is now turning into blessing and salvation. Evil does not cease to be evil. But now it is healed, and wiped away. No time is wasted considering if evil is bearable or unbearable, big or small, mortal or slight. No consideration either is given to who is deserving or not deserving. "Your Father gives his sunlight to both the evil and the good, and sends rain on the just and on the unjust" (Matt. 5). Healing and love is the banquet to which every one, friend and foe, is invited and welcome. Every parable is about the Kingdom. Every miracle is a sign of its coming. Every meal with sinners and tax collectors is proof that all are invited. "The kingdom is amongst you," said Jesus. This triumphant proclamation of Jesus is so clear for us and so fearless that it sounds like a truth which grows on every tree. But it is a frightening thing to say "Amen" to it and to mean it.

The Kingdom is amongst men as long as Christ is there. And he is always there. When men open to it they will find it and live it with Christ present there. This "Kingdom" of Jesus, of the "our Father," is certainly not a reference to heaven, or a place where the just repose. It is rather an act, an event by which God establishes justice and wipes out darkness and sin. "God's kingdom is imminent," said the Lord, "change your ways and believe in this good news" (Mark 1,15). The Kingdom is a celebration of the presence of the One who loves and always forgives and saves.

This Kingdom will grow and will permeate one's whole existence. "When man finds it," said Jesus, "for sheer joy he goes and sells everything he has and buys it" (Matt. 13).

When Christ ascended the cross he succeeded in spreading over the whole world more of himself, more of love and salvation than there will ever be of death, hatred, self centeredness and sin.

What a terrible mistake Christian churches have fallen into when they started building "moralistic defenses" and became defenders of God instead of being his heralds and announcers. Crusades and inquisitions have been a disgrace and an insult in the face of Christ. Are we today in the churches free from crusades and from waging battles for ideas and sociological conditions? Are our crusades "against depression," "against enemies," "against divorce," "against the pill," against anything that does not agree with our particular present mentality are these crusades any different in inspiration from the Crusades and Inquisitions of old!

Truth is God. Nobody can possess truth. We are possessed by truth. We do not prove or impose truth or God. We live truth and we live God. And by our way of life, Truth and God shout to others who then find them hidden in the recesses of their own souls and become possessed by them. If there could ever be criticism on the lips of those who say "our Father," it must be expressed in an artist's vision who thunders against the dullness that habit and neglect have put on the wonder of things and on the value and dignity of man.

The Christian message is a continual celebration which is designed to improve life, to give a new quality to that which already exists. It was only when the churches lost this vision that they confined themselves to moralizing and criticizing societies and individuals.

It is not necessary to believe in God to behave in life. It is not necessary to believe in God to be loyal, faithful, honest, merciful and loving. The Gospel is beyond and above moralism. The morality of the Christian is founded upon his faith in the Lord and depends on it. First you put your confidence in someone, and then you change or transform life, according to his standards. The majority of our Christian people have received "morality" before they received the good news of faith. Many still have only received morality! In fact Christians are not generally more "moral" than non Christians. The great question for humanity should be: Are they happier people because of the Good News? This is the fundamental question. Do they have faces of a people who believe in the Resurrection of Christ and in his presence in the world? Do they see in death only a moment that turns immediately into Resurrection and life everlasting, or do they see a life that ends in despair and nothingness?

The message of the Gospel could be summarized in the words of St. Paul: "Everyone moved by the Spirit is a son of God. The Spirit you received is not the Spirit of slaves bringing fear into your lives again; it is the Spirit of sons, and it makes us cry out 'Abba, Father.' The Spirit of God and our spirit bear united witness that we are children of God if only we suffer with him so as to share his glory" (Rom. 8:14-17).

CHAPTER 11

THE SEAL

The general pattern of the celebration of the sacrifice of the New Law of God in Jesus Christ is found, in its basic elements, in the sacrificial ceremony of the Old Law of Moses. The first celebration, or ceremony of worship with full ritual, is described in the ninth chapter of Leviticus. Moses divides the celebration of the people of Israel into three distinct actions: a preparation; a oblation; the coming of the fire "from before the Lord" and the consummation of the sacrifice.

Some five hundred years after Moses, Solomon carried out these same actions when he dedicated the Temple in Jerusalem. Elias the Tesbite followed the same order. And after they returned from the exile of Babylon, the people of Israel followed again the same sequence of events in their sacrifice to God. Since the purpose of this sacrifice was to placate an irate God, show repentance, and offer a reparation for sin so that the glory of the Lord might be "visible to you his people" (Lev. 9,6), a qualitative element was later added and was always exactly executed. It was the careful selection of the victim or offering the best of the flock, spotless and without blemish, the finest wheat flour, the best and costliest incense, the purest and choicest oil. At the first such offering in the desert, the people saw the glory of God and "shouted for joy and fell on their faces" (Lev. 9:24).

It is plain, therefore, that sacrifice to the Lord, to be acceptable and precious in his sight, must contain all these elements. The Last Supper of the Lord comprised them all, carefully enriched by readings and prayers taken from Holy Scripture.

The Apostles and first Christians were Jews. They were trained in the principles of Divine Worship and the splendors of the Temple. After the Ascension of the Lord, they continued to frequent the Temple and the Synagogue. Not long afterwards, persecution drove them away from the Synagogue. Frequentation of the Temple became impossible, especially after Vespasian and his cohorts destroyed it in the year 70 A.D.

Christians were left, like their brothers the Jews, without a specific place for worship. A Christian author from the second century proclaims: "We, the Christians, have no sacrifice like pagans; we have neither altars nor temples like the pagans. The only language that is pleasing to God is Thanks, Eucharist, which we express by hymns of songs of joy and recognition of his Goodness."

In their meetings Christians would read Holy Scriptures like all good Jews. They would comment on them. This was only a preparation which would be followed immediately by the commemoration of the happenings of the Last Supper, and by the repetition of the words of Christ over the Bread and Wine: "This is My Body, This is My Blood." After partaking of the Body and Blood of Christ, the assembly would then be dismissed with hymns of praise, admiration and thanksgiving for the "marvels the Lord has done to his servants." This is the Liturgy of the New Law. This is Eucharist: the celebration of thanks and praise. This liturgy is not to placate an irate God, or to repent from sin, but to experience God's glory and give him thanks and praise for his salvific deeds.

Justin, one of the first Apologists of the Christian faith, himself born shortly after the Apostles, gives an account of his faith and of the practice of the Christians of his time. He describes in detail the celebration of the Eucharist as it was conducted, and claims that these details are what the Lord himself ordered his disciples to follow. The account of the liturgy described by Justin witnesses to the details of the Sacred Supper of the Lord and harmonizes with the details of the Breaking of the Bread by the Apostles. It is this same liturgy of the first Christians that Clement of Rome describes and which the Church kept faithfully and transmitted in all its integrity. It is from this liturgy that the Byzantine Liturgy derives and has its origin.

The general construction of the sacrifice of the New Law of Christ is therefore similar to the celebration of the Old Law of Moses, of Solomon, and of generations of the Jewish people. It comprises today the threefold action described by Moses in Leviticus. There is a preparation (Prothesis), an oblation (Consecration and Epiclesis), and

Consummation (Holy Communion). In other words, the Christian assembly of today, and since the time of Christ, is united to God by the same covenant of grace and love. It is taken up into God's inner life (Anaphora or Canon). It is made ready to live the Mysteries of the goodness of God in creation and the salvific life of Christ (Anamnesis or commemorations). It vibrates to the touch of the Holy Spirit who draws every one and everything in this world and beyond this world to the Kingdom of God (Epiclesis). When, therefore, the whole world is thus sanctified, deified, and saved, every individual in the assembly surrenders himself to God so entirely in a perfect embrace of love (communion) that he overflows with joy and thanks (thanksgiving).

PREPARATION OF THE OFFERING

In the ancient Church, only the baptized, the initiated, and those instructed in the faith were allowed to bring their offerings to the altar. Bread and wine symbolize and represent those who are united to Christ and made one with him in baptism. As the many grains of wheat and the many grapes have to be crushed to become a new form of life giving element which is bread and wine, so also the baptized are grafted onto Christ and voluntarily surrendered and given to him to be one with him. Christ is the Bread of Life and the Wine of the Kingdom. Food is life and the very principle of life, and the whole world has been created as food for man. With Christ who is our bread we become a new life, life divine.

From the material offering of bread and wine of the Faithful, the deacon, and later in history, the priests, selected what was necessary for the sacrifice and used the ret of their subsistence or the subsistence of the poor. The simple ceremony of offering, receiving, selecting and distributing the bread and wine, which is the human part of the covenant, was made at a special place, or altar, called "Prothesis," or altar of offering or "Proskomedia." This ceremony became more elaborate and later developed into a short story and a condensed drama of the whole eucharistic sacrifice.

Among all the loaves offered there is one called "Prosphora" representing Christ and stamped with a seal bearing his name: "Jesus Christ the Victor," IC XC NI KA. When this seal is cut, it is called "lamb," the Lamb of God who represents here all humanity. The priest lifts up the Prosphora and signs it three times with the lance that pierced the side of the Lord on

Calvary. He cuts the seal marked with Christ's name saying:

As a sheep He was led to the slaughter.
And as a spotless lamb before the shearers He did not open His mouth
In His lowliness His judgment was taken away.
And who shall describe His generation?

The priest, thrusting the lance into the right side of the bread, lifts out the lamb, saying: "For his life was taken away from the earth." He turns it face down and pierces it on the side stamped "Jesus," saying: "One of the soldiers pierced his side with a lance." Wine is then poured into the chalice with some drops of water. The memory of Calvary becomes alive again, and the priest declares: "…and at once there came forth blood and water: and he who saw it bore witness, and his witness is true." Another special piece of bread is cut "in honor and memory of our most highly blessed and glorious Lady the Mother of God," and is placed at the right of the Lamb, for indeed "at Your right stood the Queen in an embroidered mantle of gold."

Angels, Prophets, and Saints, people living and people dead, are also represented and arranged in rows of guards around the Lamb on his throne. Through this ceremony we see the eternal sacrifice of the Son of God on the altar of heaven reproduced in the here and now. It is already a vision, a Theophany of God. The physical elements of bread and wine are filled with the Invisible. Our faith, love and prayer meet the Lord who is present and ready for his mission of salvation by which he seals his Covenant with God and with his people: "That our God who loved mankind, having received them on his holy altar in heaven as a fragrance, may send down upon us in return, his divine grace and the Holy Spirit as his gift…" (Divine Liturgy).

The priest puts a star on the oblation and declares that a "star came and stood where the Child was." He declares the faith of the assembly in the Incarnation of the Son of God and in his appearance in the human flesh. Here is Bethlehem! Even the covering of the oblation becomes an occasion for the glorification of God and for our identification with him.

The Lord King, He has clothed Himself with splendor;
The Lord has put on might and has girt Himself!
Your glory, O Christ, has covered the heavens,
And the earth is full of Your Praise.

Shelter us with the sheltering of Your wings:
Drive away from us every enemy and foe;
Grant us a peaceful life.
O Lord, have mercy on us and on your world and save our souls.

The "Sacrifice" is already present. We already call the elements of
the Divine Liturgy of Christ "sacrifice of Christ," "our sacrifice," "sacrifice of the people." Christ was alone in his suffering and offering on
the Cross. Now the people of God are present on Calvary and they have
the occasion to ratify and accept the sacrifice as their own. The point is
that we become co offerers with Christ by our obedient self giving; we
offer to God the totality of our lives, of ourselves, and of the world in
which we live. The sacrifice of Christ has been offered and accepted.
Now we make it our own and we call it "a sacrifice of praise" because
in it we recognize already the goodness and generosity of God.

After all the readings have been proclaimed, and the special celebration of the day has put the Christian in the realm of God, the official and
solemn transfer of the oblations to the main altar takes place. The transfer of the offerings is seen as the transfer of the real Christ, his entrance
to his sanctuary. The solemn procession that carries the bread and wine
is the symbol and sign of the coming of the King among his people. He
is coming among the people to gather everyone to himself and offer them
back to the Father. A stir of anticipation runs through the whole congregation. Seized by the awareness of what is going to happen, everyone falls
into a humble, yet confident, change of heart. Ministers and faithful
express sorrow for their sins and the sins of the world:

Again and many times we fall down before You and pray You in your
goodness and love for mankind to regard our supplications and cleanse
our souls and bodies from all defilement of flesh and spirit, and grant
that we may stand without guilt or condemnation before your holy altar.
And upon these also pray with us, O God, bestow increase of life and
faith and spiritual insight. Give them ever to minister to You in fear and
love, to share without guilt or condemnation in your holy mysteries and
to be made worthy of your heavenly kingdom (Byzantine Liturgy).

Purification of all sins is effected. The faithful know that they are
forgiven and sanctified. Now they can face their Redeemer and God,
unite with him and feel their complete one ness with him. They realize
that they "mystically represent the Cherubim," consequently they "put
aside all worldly care and sing their thrice holy hymn, to the King of the
universe who is coming escorted by all the angelic hosts."

Let all mortal flesh be silent;
let us stand in fear and trembling, having no other thought but the
thought of the Lord.
For behold, the King of kings and Lord of lords
is coming to be sacrificed and to be given as food to the faithful.
He is escorted by hosts of archangels
and by all the principalities and dominions.
He is indeed escorted by the many eyed Cherubim
and by the six winged Seraphim covering their faces,
All chanting: Alleluia! Alleluia! Alleluia! (673)

Preceded by candles, banners and clouds of incense, the bread and
wine are taken then into the midst of the congregation. This procession
is the sign and symbol of collecting into the unity of bread and wine
each and every one present, all the grains of wheat and the grapes of
the vine. To affirm their self surrender to Christ, everyone bows to
them and signs himself or herself in a meaningful gesture of generous
self giving.

The procession goes into the sanctuary, the Holy of holies, into
heaven as it were, where God presides on his throne surrounded with
majesty and glory. It is by ascending to heaven, by entering it, that the
Church fulfills itself, becomes what it really is: it is the "passage," the
"pesach" to heaven.

This entering is not a symbol. "It is the crucial and decisive act in which
the true dimensions of the sacrament are revealed and established"
(Schmemann). The Bishop and all his priests surround the altar. They realize that they are to perform the holiest and most sacred act of religion.
Face to face with God, they realize the awesomeness of his holiness. They
proclaim his goodness and beg for admittance to his presence. At his
transfiguration on Mount Thabor, the Lord did not change into some
other form. He simply opened the inner eyes of his Apostles to make
them capable of seeing, through his physical body, what he really was in
himself. He was light and bliss. And they finally really saw.

Here again, the Lord opens the inner eyes of our faith and makes us
capable of seeing his salvific redemption already present in the bread
and in the wine. With a deep sentiment of humility, we bow our heads
and ask the Holy Spirit to descend upon us, upon the gifts and upon all
the people, and accept their offerings as a sacrifice of praise and glory:

Lord God Almighty, who alone are holy, who accept the sacrifice of praise from those who call upon You with their whole heart, accept also the prayer of us sinners and carry it to your holy altar; make us fit to offer You spiritual gifts and sacrifices for our sins and the faults of the people. Make us worthy to find grace in your eyes, that our sacrifice may become acceptable to You, and that the good Spirit of your grace may abide with us and with the gifts here laid out and with all your people (280).

THE ROYAL DOORS

A cry rises loud and clear: "The Doors! The Doors!" The Royal Doors are then closed and the curtain drawn shut. The opening and closing of doors are significant actions in man's life, a part of the ebb and flow of life. A great mystery lies in doors. They hide or reveal what is inside and keep the heart in suspense. They are symbols of privacy, of retreat, of the mind's escape into quietude or sad secret struggle, or joyous encounter. "Heaven without doors is not heaven," say the mystics, "it is a hallway." Closing a door may signify finality, or weakness, or a tragic happening of life. The closing of doors is a mystic act.

The ministers and the gifts are now hidden from the world, and inaccessible to human inspection. Like Moses on Mount Sinai, all ministers are completely immersed in the vision and contemplation of a heavenly intercourse with God himself. "No one can look at my face and stay alive," said the Lord. It is regrettable that the closing of the doors at this moment has been marred and almost neglected in most churches. It is a lack of understanding and appreciation of the real meaning of the most awesome moment and action of our Christian religion!

The more secularized we become, the more our vision of the sacred and the holy becomes blurry, and even blinded. The closing of the Doors and curtains is not setting apart the clergy as if in a special class, shunning the people of God from participation. Participation in the Mysteries cannot be realized by physical contact, but only by words and personal gestures that create an inner vision and plunge the whole man into the reality of the invisible and mysterious.

The sanctuary and altar have been, throughout the spiritual development of the Church, gradually hidden and separated, not by an ecclesiastical, bureaucratic mandate, but by the Christian sense of the sacred, by the real sense of the awesomeness of the mystery of God. St. John Chrysostom and all the Fathers constantly call the altar the "Terrifying table," and the mystery of the altar "Terrifying Mysteries," "the terrifying sacrifice of the Body and Blood of Christ to which we have to approach with fear and trembling." This is sacred "terror" and not fear of the unknown. It is a mystic trembling in the presence of heaven: "Take off your shoes," said God, "for the place where you stand is holy" (Exodus 3:5).

The shutting of the Doors and the keeping of the altar of sacrifice hidden from physical sight is not a hindrance to participation. It is rather a forceful revelation that there is a mystery, and that we cannot see or experience this mystery by physical contact. No human eyes or physical sight can penetrate contact. No human eyes or physical sight can penetrate it or comprehend it. Only love and the surge of the soul on the wings of faith can meet the Lord and God of all. "We celebrate the Mysteries with closed doors and keep out the uninitiated," says Chrysostom, "not that we are ashamed of our rites, but that many are still imperfectly prepared for them." The lines and colors of the Iconostasis purify the vision of the initiated and believers and help them penetrate into the invisible for the contemplation and adoration of the divine Mystery. The closed Doors are a sign and symbol of a distinction, not a separation.

There are here three completely different states of being and consequently three different roles to be played: the ministers of the altar, Christ mysteriously present, and the people of God. The Holy Spirit acts on the ministers; Christ acts on the elements and on the ministers. Once the oblations have acquired a new meaning and reality, they will affect the people. The ministers here do not represent the assembled congregation as they did in the first part of the celebration. They represent now the person of Christ, risen and offering his eternal worship in heaven. They are "in heaven" with Christ.

The people are awaiting the descent of the Holy Spirit upon the sacrificial elements and the descent of Christ himself into them. They are expecting the opening of the Doors and are looking forward to seeing heaven open to earth, deluging it with life, joy and salvation. Heaven is hidden from their eyes now. But the revelation will soon burst out at the opening of the Doors which will reveal the unknown. Opening a door is an act as mystic as its closing. It gives a sense of moving into a new pattern of human life. Opening the Holy Doors includes the highest glimpse of heavenly gladness, reunion, reconciliation, bliss of lovers too long parted.

THE KISS OF PEACE AND CREED

The sign and seal of the love of God is the love of neighbor. After having obtained forgiveness from God and making our peace with him, we ask now forgiveness from each other and we forgive each other. The Ministers proclaim to all: "Let us love one another." Every one present confesses and proclaims his unity with Christ, the Lover of men. "I will love you, Lord my strength. The Lord is my fortress, my refuge, and my deliverance!" Because of the love of the Lord who fills us with his peace and joy, we overflow with love. And because we know that Christ has forgiven us, we feel the urgent desire to forgive others and to be at peace with them. Each member of the assembly enthusiastically embraces his neighbor and gives the Kiss of Christ saying: "Christ is in our midst." And the other answers: "He is and he always will be!"

What a marvelous reality! Christians cannot hide or forget their all embracing love. The Church, to be the Church of Christ, has to be first the revelation of that divine love which God "poured into our hearts." Without this love, nothing is valid in the Church. The kiss of Christ is the dynamic sign wherein Christians express their love for each other before they share the one bread. Christ is our real love and life and our forgiveness. We share him with others. Breaking the bread of Christ becomes a little vacuous without the breaking open of ourselves. It is Christ who unites us to one another and through one another to God.

Once the brotherly love of forgiving is secure, the whole assembly bursts into singing the glory of the Trinity, by singing the Creed. This was composed in the year 325 at Nicea on the occasion of that Council. It fixed in human words the content of faith and its proclamation.

We use the Creed in our prayers several times a day. Not as a formula of belief any more, but as an acceptance and proclamation of the love and life of the Holy Trinity in whom we plunge and find ourselves. For us, "God Creator" is not a superman or a magic performer but an Artist, a Worker, and Inventor and Maker of things and Producer of life. Since God is a Worker Artist, all of his creation is good. The Son is a Savior and a Lover. "For us men and for our salvation," He lived, died, resurrected, ascended all will come back again. The Holy Spirit is Life and Giver of life and eternal joy. A Christian refuses to recite a formula or belief in dogmas. A Christian does not believe in intellectual representations or dogmas. He believes in divine facts. The affirmation of the facts that display to our heart and reality of the three divine

Persons is a strength that flows into our soul like a river feeding a parched land. We sink into it.

In reciting the Creed, we plunge into life, the life of God who is Father, Son and Holy Spirit. With symbolic penetration we show that our self confident thinking and living is built not on a hollow shell, but on the solid rock of Christ who "descended" into Hades, into the inaccessible foundations of life, to rescue the world. The fact that the Father is "Creator," an Artist, brings us to the fact that the Son is a Lover.

The fact of Christ brings us naturally to the fact of the Holy Spirit who is Life giver, who makes death merge into resurrection and resurrection into eternal life. Christians who proclaim in the Creed their acceptance of life in God, Father Son Holy Spirit, enter into the realm of creation, into the Kingdom of heaven, and become ready to respond to God's excellence and love in the accomplishment of the mysteries soon to become reality on the altar. The proclamation of the Creed is not, therefore, the recitation of a formula, or a list of dogmas. It is the celebration of the facts of the divine life. Outside of these facts Christians only find a void, because by themselves they are immersed in their own existence which is like a shadow that slips into nothingness and dissolves like rain.

Within the reality expressed by the Creed we find ourselves living and moving in an infinite and unmeasured Being who is Father and tenderness, who is Son, and Lover, who is Spirit and Life giver. It is the glory of the Christian to declare that all these facts were planned and executed by God not for God's sake but "for us men and for our salvation." We were redeemed, not because of our success or our mature years, but because of our troubles and perils and God's greater love for us. In these facts then, we find rebirth in death, resurrection, and life eternal. We are ready to go deeper into the realities of God and become "eucharistic."

CHAPTER 12

THE CHRISTIAN

Every person is made in the image and likeness of God. We are essentially religious, always searching for our real roots, for that original image of God in us, always longing to see the face of God either to affirm him or to negate him. The Christian shares with every person the same movement of intelligence and understanding to affirm God and to admire his goodness. Another movement the Christian shares with everyone who professes belief in God is that all stand in awe before the majesty of man and creation in which they read the name of God and proclaim him. They all witness that this God is the principle of all beauty and love. From him everything came to be. To him everything must return in an upward movement of love and admiration and praise.

Christians have yet another characteristic. Since we are baptized in Christ, we bear Christ, we are "Christophers." We share in the reality of the Person of Christ, in his priesthood, and in his divine immolation by which Christ sanctifies, divinizes and gives salvation to the whole universe. Christians are therefore always alive to God and always listening to his presence in themselves, in nature, and in others. They are ever ready to move with the impulse of the Holy Spirit into the sphere of their divine roots and into the sanctifying and sanctified realities which are the true realities of this world. Christ is its reality. Christians therefore see in the world the sacrament of Christ's presence, the growth of the Kingdom and of life eternal.

BAPTIZED

At baptism one is robed in white. The color white is the symbol and sign of freedom and it proclaims kingship. Man is robed in the likeness of God, the supremely free and supremely King. White means precisely freedom and not a moral virtue of conduct. The Christian is king. He is free from all contingencies that fetter or enslave. He was created to transform the world into the Kingdom of God. In baptism, man is restored to the power of true human nature, to "original" creation. He was created to proclaim God's activity and to celebrate God's deeds, not only in creation but in human life and human history. God the Son became man to unite us and creation to God the Father and to restore everything to its pristine dignity and beauty.

At the Incarnation, Christ became the center of unity, of harmony and cohesion for all creation. All creatures past, present and future depend upon him for their existence, and they cannot be fully understood if their relationship with him is broken: "In him they were created." When God became man he opened space and time to the Holy Spirit who penetrated them with the fullness of his divine presence. The Holy Spirit fills them, and thus makes them elements of unity for all humanity. Time and space are no longer elements of separation. They become the atmosphere of the breath of God where the Christian can reach others, at all times and places. "In Christ everything in heaven and on earth was created. Not only things visible but also invisible…the whole universe has been created through him and for him. He exists before everything and all things are held together in Him" (Col. 1:16-17).

In baptism, therefore, Christ becomes a fact, an intimate, personal and interior fact in the baptized: "My hands," says St. Symeon, "are the hands of a wretched man. But when I move my hand, my hand is all Christ." In his baptism the Christian becomes one with Christ, a carrier of Christ, a "Christopher." Consequently, he carries also the whole of creation to sanctify it by the Holy Spirit of Jesus who dwells in him and acts through him. Christians are agents and sharers in this divine action. It is in Christ that Christians find their divine dimension, their all embracing humanity and their cosmic immensity. In Christ, there is but one man, and the cosmos is the body of humanity. The cosmos is the first Bible and the language that God uses to enter into relation with man.

CONFIRMATION

If at baptism Christians become one with Christ, in confirmation they are "sealed with the gift of the Holy Spirit." The Seal or "gift of the Holy Spirit" is not a thing or a quality different from the divine

Person of the Holy Spirit. It is the Spirit himself, the Gift of the Father, the Sent of the Son who "takes over" in the Christian, who in turn becomes carrier of the Holy Spirit, "Pneumatophor."

The Spirit enters life to envelop it with fire and love, filling everything with joy and hope. In the Byzantine celebration of confirmation the "Seal of the Holy Spirit" is still given not only on the forehead, which represents the whole of the human being indeed, but also on the eyes, on the nose, on the ears, on the mouth, on the breast, on the hands and on the feet. Every member and every sense of the human body becomes fire and light and a source radiating fire and life to everything and everyone. Each member of the body becomes a carrier of the Spirit and a sanctifier with the Sanctifier. The Christian breathes life and salvation with the breath of God. "You have been stamped with the seal of the Holy Spirit...You whom God has taken for his own to make his glory praised" (Eph. 1:13-14).

It is the essential function of the Holy Spirit to communicate what Christ possesses in himself, to extend to all creation what is unique and personal in Christ, and to impart to creation the sublime character of Christ. Through the baptized, the Spirit includes also each and every one in the intimate relation that binds Christ to the Father.

Furthermore, when the baptized receives the Body and Blood of the Lord he becomes, in the words of St. Cyril of Jerusalem, "one flesh" with Christ, his blood is mingled and becomes "one blood with Christ." He is really "Christified" and Child of the Father. And Nicolas Cabazilas adds: "The mud receives royal dignity...and is transformed into the substance of the King..." And St. Sergius of Radonezh of the fourteenth century summarizes it all:

Baptized in the fire.
Illumined by the Spirit
Whoever you are
You are the throne of God
You are his dwelling Place and his instrument
You are the light and the divinity You are God
God! God! God!

PEACE MAKER

The Christian is therefore king, priest and prophet. He is by his spiritual mastery over his nature. He keeps his head high above all the contingencies of life, and maintains a bright sunshine in his heart. He is free in himself. He is king because he is free in his active mastery of the universe, not to destroy it, but to commune with it, to bless, transform, and sanctify it. He is free because he submits himself to every form of life in order to make it grow and expand. He is king by inspiring justice and peace in the events of his society. He is king and free by the very fact of being self crucified presence by which he liberates others. For the Christian, the crown of thorns is a crown of redeeming fire.

The Christian is a priest because he breathes in God. He breathes the Holy Spirit and thus makes the whole universe and man breathe in God. His respiration is a prayer, a power to turn everything into a hymn of praise. "He stands in the center of the world and unifies it in his act of blessing God by both receiving the world from God and offering it back to God and by filling the world with this Eucharist, he transforms his life, the one that he receives from the world, into life in God, into communion" (Schmemann).

The Christian is also a prophet of respect for every human value, for every human being. Since God became a human face, every human face is a holy face. The Christian knows that he cannot put his brother in communion with God unless he first enters into communion with his brother. He knows that he has to love his brother, not only for what he is, but much more for what he is destined to be. His first concern, therefore, is to be at "peace" with him.

The liturgy never tires of reminding the Christian of the necessity of this peace. "In peace let us pray…" "For peace from on high and for peace in the whole world…" "That our life be peaceful…" "That the end of our life be peaceful…" "Peace to you all…" The fruit of peace is joy. The vision of peace is an all embracing vision, because it is the hallmark of the presence of Christ.

Peace derives directly from the Spirit of God and was the legacy of our Lord at the hour of his departure: "Peace I leave with you, my peace I give to you…" (John 14:27). For Christ to speak of peace is essentially to impart it. Peace is the shared glory of the Resurrection by which Christ becomes the center of our life, our reconciliation with God, and the abiding harmony in the events of life.

One finds Christ when he enters into this peace. And to desire such a peace is to follow, knowingly or unknowingly, the footsteps of Christ. "Blessed are the peacemakers, for they are children of God" (Matt. 5:9). Peace is not something. It is Christ himself working, inspiring, living and loving. Wishing peace, giving peace, means offering Christ himself as a gift and as the presence of his person. Christ lives in his gift. His gift is himself which "surpasses all understanding." Where peace is, therefore, Christ is, and the human heart has passed from searching to repose, from asking to finding, from desire to possession. The fire of desire, of restlessness and anxiety becomes maturity, security and joy.

Peace gathers what life scatters. Like the rainbow, the sign of God's peace after the deluge, it hovers over the contradictions of life. The alien is made a friend, what was torn is made whole, wounds are healed. It brings reconciliation into a world of contradictions, and through it the forces of unity triumph over the world wide forces of disruption. Amid breakdowns and failures it gives a foretaste of ultimate success. It is the harbinger of the perfection to come (Biser, *The Light of the Lamb*).

The Church's prayer is incessantly reminding its faithful of this life giving peace because it is not a mere word but a deep reality and a prayer: "And may the peace of God which surpasses all understanding guard your hearts and your minds in Christ Jesus" (Phil. 4:7). The litany of all the intentions of the Christian is called a "litany of peace," because whatever the Christian says or does serves others and brings them to where he has come, to the light and joy which is the peace of Christ.

SACRAMENT OF THE BROTHER

Some writers too easily dismiss Christian spirituality as being "spiritual," and not concerned with society. For Christians, and especially for Eastern and later Byzantine Christians, "spiritual" and "spirituality" are realities deeply connected with the "social." To be "spiritual" is not to withdraw to a more "holy place" as superficial commentaries on Christian life would have us believe. Withdrawal was and is still only a means to becoming a more prayerful person, to change injustice to justice, and be more dedicated to the realization of the Kingdom. A spiritual power is a power to motivate and incite us to larger visions that our culture possesses.

St. John Chrysostom writes the most amazing pages on the Incomprehensibility of God, but he connects his doctrine with the personal experience of society and the "sacrament of the brother." One of the reasons for his own condemnation by others was that he "sold sacred vessels to give money to the poor." The man who prays must give. He gives to his brother who is the "Sacrament of Christ." Because he looks after his brother, he will see the face of God.

Furthermore, Chrysostom and many Fathers of Eastern spirituality courageously opposed the powers of emperors in the name of freedom and liberty of conscience. They even throw doubts on private property in favor of the destitute; they reject inheritance for the sake of the deprived. Asceticism is intimately allied to this "spiritual" involvement. Asceticism is the "invisible fight," relentless and always in pain, for one's self and for others. Asceticism has indeed a negative aspect which is a self renouncement and a continual watch. These are means, not ends. They aim at illumination and the acquisition of the gifts of the Holy Spirit in order to know one's self: "No one can come to know God if he does not know himself" (Philokalia). And St. Isaac proclaims: "He who recognizes his sins is greater than the one who has seen the angels."

Asceticism aims to change all the passions into powerful energies of patience, love, openness to God and to the "brother," and to develop one's God given talents to become an artist, scientist or a saint. Asceticism clothes the Christian with the fiery and all consuming presence of God so that it overflows in love for the other. The prayer of the Christian is not to escape from this world to another world of joy and bliss. It is a remembrance of the Father who so loved the world that he gave his only Begotten Son. It is a remembrance of the Incarnation which plunges us into the world for its transformation. It is a remembrance also of the Holy Spirit who enables us to love with the love of Christ. The prayer which blinds us to injustice and tends to other worldliness is sterile prayer.

This vision of the praying Christian is most explicitly clarified in the "Litany of Peace" which opens all Byzantine public prayers and some Western liturgies also. In this litany the Christian gathers within himself the public servants, authorities both religious and civil; cities, country places and all those who live in them; the travelers by sea, land, and air; the sick and those who suffer and those forgotten brothers who are in prisons. The Christian lives deeply in touch with the troubles of the world and feels the pain of human life intensely. He brings all the earth, and whatever it contains, to God for his mercy, and dedicates himself for its healing and welfare.

This litany of intentions is the vibrant acclamation of the Christian that everything and everyone belongs to God's kingdom, where saint and sinner, believer and unbeliever, are at home, and where all share in the peace of God. The praying Christian realizes here that he is the brother of all and responsible for all. For him, "There is no question here of Greek or Jew, circumcised or uncircumcised, barbarian, Scythian, freeman or slave; but Christ is all and is in all" (Col. 3:11). The prayer of the Christian is not only a proclamation; it is the affirmation of his responsibility and true relation with the world. It makes him go beyond himself and accept all that challenges of his society, whether religious or civil.

PRAYERFUL

Religious education does not consist in imparting "knowledge" about God, but in the revelation of the wonderful things that happen continually in the divine gift of the "New Life" of the Christian. In this new life, man and the world become really what God meant them to be: the gift of God to man and the means of man's communion with God Prayer for the Christian means to "be together, in the company of God," "to associate with," "to be friends." The Ancients devised a prayer, a cry of the heart, by which they meant to awaken the dormant and stir up the indifferent to this new reality of man and of the world. The "Kyrie eleison," "Lord have mercy!" is a cry in the night: "Wake up!" It proclaims the universality of the embrace of Christ which the Christian makes his own.

The mercy of God is the outpouring of love and goodness that sanctify and divinize. The mercy of God is not a "condescension," a paternalism, on the part of God, "a crumb that falls from the Master's table." The mercy of God is God himself in his transforming presence. It is he, the Bread broken for all, generously given and completely sur-rendered. The mercy of God is the life giving perpetuation of that divine energy of the Redeemer's love. The cry of "Lord, have mercy," therefore, invokes the divine presence upon the whole of creation, upon mankind and matter, upon the whole world thought of as gathered in the one embrace of Christ. It is invoked upon the invisible creation as well as upon those now on earth, and upon those whose life here has ended; in short, upon all that makes up cosmos, sub human and angel-ic (Oakley, *The Orthodox Liturgy*). The "Lord have mercy" rings out after every intention the Christian mentions.

Many are the needs. Many, therefore, are the cries for mercy. The rhythm of intention and the repetition of the "Lord, have mercy" is the manifestation of the all embracing concern of Christ's and of the

Christian's heart. It teaches the individual and the community their true relation with the world and with all men as it makes them go beyond themselves to embrace the whole world, men and events, and carry them in their prayer and in their daily life.

Every prayer, as every act of the Christian, is ordained ultimately not only to his own fulfillment in the "vision of God" in heaven, but also to the transformation and consummation of all things in Christ. In Christ, all that is full of possibilities for beauty, truth, community and justice. And the Christian is vowed to draw out all these possibilities into the realities of this world. All of reality invites him to respond to goodness with goodness of his own. The swaying and sounds and whispers of nature and of man are a continual prayer that brings God to man. The Christian hears within his soul these cries and sighs and longing, and he brings them in an upward movement of praise and glory to God.

The recitation of the litany of intentions is an exemplification of the Christian's answer to the command of the Lord to "love one another as I have loved you." Here the Christian goes beyond the shores of his limited personal interests and enlarges the embrace of his love to all the members of the human family. His heart and his concern carry the weak and the strong, kings and bishops, those who are in authority and those whoa re bedridden, sick, prisoners, and especially those who are exposed to the dangers of life, the travelers and wayfarers. He gathers them in his heart and brings them all to the feet of God, as to their Father.

The entire material creation is also remembered and offered to God that it may be a source of joy and security for man. Prayers are offered for "good and favorable weather," "abundance of the fruits of the earth," and all that is necessary for order and "peace in this world." This is the kingdom of God! "Blessed is the kingdom of the Father and of the Son and of the Holy Spirit…"

ALL EMBRACING

What is exclusive and particularly proper to the Baptized is that in his prayer he bears with him the whole universe. He is a "priest." As a member of Christ, he is not a lonely individual. He is a society and represents society; he summarizes this universe in its entirety and embraces it in his adoring love. We can say that the litany of intentions which the Christian utters embodies the ground of unity and the harmony in diversity of our "various gifts" (1 Cor. 12:4). Priests, deacons and people together sing the "we" of the community: "Let us pray to the Lord." When Christians assemble to offer themselves, the whole creation is thus offered. When two or three are gathered in the name of Christ, Christ said that he will be present with them to pray and adore and share all their intentions and their doings. The "Shekina," the glory of God, shines through the assembly.

The anchorite in his solitude and the isolated monk, as well as the person who is caught up in the daily whirlwind of life, all participate in the prayer of the assembly, even when they are not directly involved in it. This is one of the reasons why those who do not attend public prayers and liturgies, even on Sundays, are not condemned. They are not liable to "mortal sin" for their absence. They are present and included in those representing them in the community of God, in the "two or three who are gathered in his Name."

Holy Silouan expresses this idea in a simple, yet highly theological way: "The love of Christ being a divine force and a gift of the Holy Spirit, the one Spirit acting universally, makes all men ontologically one. Love takes to itself the life of the loved one. The man who loves God is drawn into the life of the Godhead; he who loves his brother draws his brother's life into his own hypostatic being. The one who loves the whole world in the Spirit will embrace the whole world." When he comes into the presence of God, he brings with him the whole world.

The Christian spreads his wings over the whole world. He even assumes the evil of the world. He goes through the agony of Gethsemane and ascends to the vision that enlightens his whole being and enables him to see his brother as he really is, a child of God, a member of Jesus Christ. He is pure of heart "When one sees all other men as good and no one is impure in his eyes, then we can say that he is enthusiastically 'pure of heart.'" "When you see your brother committing a sin, throw over him the mantle of your love," says Saint Isaac in his sentences. "All asceticism that lacks love for the brother," say our spiritual Fathers, "all asceticism which is not the 'sacrament of the brother,' is vain." Abbot Poemen always refused to punish his monks: "When I see a brother going to sleep at the divine office, I place his head on my knee and let him peacefully go to sleep" (Apophthegmata).

Faith is personal, a personal opening to God's word and a personal acceptance of God's invitation. The expression of faith is the search for a person and not for a thing. It is the encounter of two lovers, one descending, God, and one ascending, man.

PRAYER OF THE PSALMS

There is a body of prayer which the Christian cherishes and loves and which in turn nourishes and enlightens him, the psalms. The Christian realizes that in prayer it is God who invites him and enters into his very being and lays hold of him. The prayer of the psalms realizes this invitation better than any other prayer.

The people of Jesus Christ, Israel, saw themselves, their Exodus, and their whole history as a nation in these psalms. In time of joy as in time of trouble, they took the psalms to themselves, and they became the one man who thus prayed to God.

Jesus, who is the distillation of Israel's vocation, prayed these same psalms throughout his life. They are the very words that he used in speaking with his Father as he spent the night "in prayer to God." If one opens his heart to their meaning, if he opens his being to the experience they embody, his soul will move in rhythm with the soul of Christ who is still praying them in his Church and in all mankind. Christ prays them in us if we are willing to accept the experience and responsibility of our union with him. But, unlike the people of the Old Law, the Christian recognizes that he has no more "enemies." He does not wish evil or destruction towards any "evil doer," nation, or individual. He is the one man who is carrying out from one end of the world's history to the other the suffering and darkness of mankind and sharing his unconquerable hope of God's power to save and to heal. The Christian is a savior with the Savior. He does not and cannot wish death or destruction to others.

In time of trouble and joy, Jews and Christians alike use the songs of the psalms to praise and worship the God of their fathers. In Christian monasteries like those of Pachomius, it was prescribed as a condition for entering religious life that a man should know by heart the Gospels and the text of the psalms.

It is obvious that in the prayer of a Christian, the very same thought is often repeated, and in many ways. Psalms and doxologies are repeated every day, several times a day, and in the same office. Repetition is the way of man's spirit. The constant repetition of a particular prayer in every act of worship is a confident cry of love. Repetition is both active and passive involvement in God. It is the gift of oneself and the whole cosmos, and a welcome offered by one's whole being to God. Repetition is an act of love, always repeated and ever new. Repetition expands consciousness.

A short, oft-repeated prayer is called, in Western language, a "spiritual ejaculation," an "arrow" which is destined to hit a target and stick to it. Ejaculations have no meaning unless they prepare for and introduce the wondrous happening: hitting the target. The repetition of such a prayer should therefore increase our yearning for the realization or the manifestation of the Kingdom of God. Those participating in Divine Worship repeat short prayers often. It is therefore a glaring absurdity to hurry over them. We should leave room for real deep breathing in order to increase the conscious realization of God.

This is the same psychological principle that explains and justifies the "Jesus Prayer." Just as a pebble dropped into a pond causes an endless series of ripples, so these short prayers, repeated again and again, reach from the center of our soul to its shores, calming them by their touch and washing them by their peaceful lull. The repetition must therefore be slow, eager, and loud, or silent and meditative. I remember as a child the impression the old monks made upon me by the way they sang and sighed and groaned their prayers. The depth of feeling and the sincerity of spontaneity they expressed in them made the prayers sound like a mystical incantation that led to a communication with the Invisible where one finds himself in the infinite ocean of God.

PRAYER AND DESIRE

The Christian can also pray for seemingly very secondary things like success, health, weather, the welfare of a friend, and for innumerable other personal intentions. But the Christian understands, at the same time, that this kind of prayer is not individualistic. His many intentions in prayer show that he is full of desires. He always overflows with hope in the presence of God. He is never satisfied. He perpetually dreams of better things to come. The predominance of science in the Western world has gradually relegated the prayer of petition to a status of superstition. The prayer of asking, of begging, is a commitment to listen to God, to others, to their needs and hopes. St. Thomas Aquinas said that "by prayer man renders himself capable of receiving" (II, c. 2). The confidence of a Christian in God is like the requests of a child who is always bent on personal desires: give me water, food, a doll, rain, sunshine or snow. A child is a dependent person. He asks to have an answer, any answer. Why? Just because!

When the child grows out of dependence he will accept his own responsibility and give himself to the whisper of a lover who is there not to do but to be with us. By his or her presence the person will be supported and encouraged in doing what he must do.

Desire is kin to adoration. Adoring and desiring are necessary for life. He who has no desire is a man asleep, a corpse moving through the torrent of life. He has no hope. Christianity is a religion of desire, and of hope against hope. Desire overcomes death to find real life. Christ taught us "to ask and to knock," and to pray for our "daily bread." According to modern biblical scholars, this "daily bread" does not refer only to daily needs. It is not a magical request or a type of commercial bartering, a tit for tat. It is the desire for a loving presence. It refers primarily to the coming banquet of the Kingdom which is man's bread of tomorrow, of the future. It Is the bread the Christian hopes to share with his brothers in the coming kingdom and he asks for it "today." What a freedom! "Seek first the kingdom and his justice, and everything else will be given to you" (Matt. 6:33). If one does not hope, he will never find the impossible.

Among all founders of religions, Christ is the only one who does not suppress desires. He is the only one who preaches "satisfaction." Mohammed talks about resignation. Islam means precisely that, "surrender," "submission," which is still a noble attitude in the presence of God. But it does suppress human desire. Buddha and Socrates teach how to stifle all desires. Christ teaches us to hunger and thirst for "bread," and for "living water," and for dignity, and for love, and for friendship, and above all for justice and goodness, which means for God himself. God only gives his bread to the one who asks for it. The poor are declared "blessed" because of their needs and their desires to satisfy them. God is over us as a Father. He is beside us as a Brother. He is in us as an Abyss that can never be filled, always giving more life and hunger for the plenitude of life. Plenitude is not virtue, moralism, or blind obedience, but a cry of confidence and of love coming out of the depth of one's heart.

"The best evangelization of the world, the most effective testimony the Christian can produce, is that exploding song, a doxology of glorification that rises from the very womb of the earth through which blows the mighty breath of the consoler, the Paraclete who alone can convert and heal" (Evodokimov, *Sacrament de l'Amour*). This is the nobility and the grandeur of the Christian and the Christian's calling and raison d'etre.

THE DEATH OF THE CHRISTIAN

For the Christian, even death is a celebration. Through all the anguishes of our life, all the absurdities of the world, through all horrors, all desperations, we see the light of Christ shining because Christ is risen and he is alive. He is all. He is in all. All is in him. In him the children of Rachel are risen, and Lazarus springs up out of his grave; and the little boy is raised from death and given back to his mother; the adulteress proudly spreads her silky hair to the wind and Peter is forgiven.

For the Christian, death is only an "exit." The Christian abandons the shackles and confinements of time and space and opens to glory. Glory, according to St. Paul, is a reality that transforms the material body into a spiritual body, very similar to the body of Christ at his own resurrection. Glory is the radiance and majestic splendor, which surrounds God and accompanies him, and which will likewise surround and accompany Jesus when he comes in his Second Coming on the clouds of heaven.

This is the death of the Christian. The caterpillar comes out of its cocoon and deposits on the ground its empty shell, to become a butterfly. The bright silky robe of the beloved is hung in the closet and reminds the lover of a past evening long swallowed by eternity. Life is not taken away. It is transformed.

The funeral service of a Christian reminds us of all these realities, and more. Christ has conquered evil and death. Not a single form of life or action can escape his radiance. Redemption transforms man and covers with a mantle of glory his "mantle of skin" (St. Gregory) and whatever sin clings to it.

God loved the world in its "state of sin." The victory of the Son of God breaks all frontiers, all separations and boundaries. His dynamic action extends even to hell. "He descended into hell," we keep on repeating. Christ makes perfect whatever has been broken by the fall, and he manifests his saving love without reservation. Christianity is, therefore, the hope of the final success of the cosmos against all the limits of time and space that seek to corrode it. This is the resurrection of the flesh, or, as we call it in the Creed, "the life to come."

What gives beauty to this hope is that the leaving behind of time and space will not destroy the essence of matter. Matter is an essential part of the human personality. Plato was therefore wrong by asserting that heaven is only for the "soul." It is a "banquet," a "wedding," a "vineyard." It is for men, for the whole man, body and soul, matter and spirit.

In Christ everything is full of angels, of life, of hope. Everything and everyone has a new beginning. There is no more death since death itself is full of God. "Christ crushes death by his death," and he goes down to hell to come out of it as "out of a royal nuptial chamber." He faces his persecutors with pardon and resurrection. He offers to everyone the gift of "son ship of God" and an immortality that begins even in this life.

The real death the Christian fears and avoids is the death of the heart which makes people indifferent to the other. This death is forgetfulness, forgetting that God exists, that my brother exists, and consequently that one exists himself. This death is satanical.

In the perspective of the Fathers of the Church, death and hell are not at the end of this life, a state of being beyond the tomb. Death and hell refer to a separated existence here on earth, the contradictions of life, its anguishes and fears which estrange man from himself. Death and hell are, in reality, time that drowns and destroys. It is the space that separates, alienates and imprisons man. It is, finally, a certain hatred of self that makes one hate others and turn them into strangers and opponents. Death, which is the end of time and space, is in reality life and eternity!

"He has passed to real life where there is no pain, no sorrow, no sighing, but life that has no limit." The celebration of death goes on to describe martyrs and saints and angels of God singing the triumphant "Alleluia" because they encounter their Lover, Christ, and Christ encounters in the one dead "the lover of Christ," as says the same liturgy. Every Christian on his death bed is or becomes a "lover of Christ," because he has been snatched from the power of darkness and transplanted into the Kingdom of light and everlasting sound of joy." "Alleluia!"

In the Byzantine ceremony of death, great lyrics describe how life and death dramatize the work of Christ. Christ's work is a work of salvation, of forgiveness and a banquet a wedding where the dead one enters with full confidence because he sees heaven standing open to him. The celebration of death at the funeral service describes God as the Judge whose role is to set aside evil and condemnation and melt away every sin and transgression the Christian might have committed during his life time. From the eternal silent lips of God comes back the word that recreates the "original image and the first creation:"

O God of all spirits and of all flesh,

You have destroyed death.

You overcame the devil and gave life to the world.

Grant now, O Lord, to the soul of your servant, who just departed from this life,

That he may rest in a place of light, of happiness,

In a place of peace where there is no grief, no sorrow, no pain. Since you are gracious, God and Lover of Men,

Forgive him every sin he has committed

By thought, or word, or deed,

For there is no man who lives and does not sin.

You alone are without sin.

Your goodness is everlasting and your word is true.

You are the resurrection, the life and the repose of your servant. Our God is the God of faithfulness and he cannot disown himself Alleluia!

CHAPTER 13

THE EUCHARISTIC CHRISTIAN

Along with the Christian, the whole of creation enters into the intimate and ultimate reality of God. World and life are going to be transformed into a new world and into a new life. All the covenants that God ever made with Noah and creation, with Abraham and his generation, with Moses and his people, with Jesus Christ and the whole universe, are going to be made one, manifest and present in all their dimensions and in the fullness of their meaning.

The "Memorial" of the Lord means that past events are now renewed in all their effectiveness. The matter of the universe, symbolized in the offerings of bread and wine, becomes the Body and Blood of God, and the Christian becomes "eucharistic." He blazes with gratitude and thanks for the present realization of salvation and divinization which the Trinity had decreed from all eternity. This is the holiest part of the divine celebration of the Christian religion. This is the Anaphora or canon.

The Christian has no more time to think of God "against the material world," or "against man," or of "man set up against God." The truth of Christianity is the truth of the divine humanity, that God became matter to purify it and save it. He became man so that man might become God. In Christ present in the matter, God reveals himself to man and man opens himself to God and accepts him. This is the marvelous truth of Christianity; this is the exchange of lives. The face of God in man, the face of man in God.

The offerings of bread and wine and are now "lifted up" from the earthly place to the divine and holy altar of God in heaven, thereby uniting the two. In this action of lifting up, the whole creation finds its way to God who pours out on it the same love he has for his Son. Salvation is thus made present and real. The Church also becomes real. She is seen to be what she really is, "the Bride of Christ," pure and undefiled.

The Anaphora or Canon remembers and expresses in its reality a double movement, one of descent and one of ascent. In the first movement, God descends upon man and creation to "lift them up" and make them sharers in his divine life. This movement is called a "mercy of peace." The mercy of God is the gift of God, his self-revelation and self-giving. The second movement is a movement of ascent. Man is taken up to God to offer him praise and thanks. This movement of ascent is called "sacrifice of praise."

Man offers all he has. All he has is thanks and praise. This is the answer of man to the gift of God, his awareness and recognition of God's goodness. The tremendous mystery of the power, condescension and infinite love of God of "descending" and "lifting up" is enacted on the altar in these two successive and dynamic movements by which creation and man are deified. This mystery will culminate in the final and decisive union of the Creator with his creature in Holy Communion.

Christianity is essentially a religion of remembrance. It remembers, renews, and celebrates every gesture God made for the good of man. It is always alive to God's marvelous deeds of love and goodness and to love the divine value of the human person. To remember is to love. God remembers us and we remember him. We remember in particular the sacrifice of Christ as a past event of suffering and death which becomes now on the altar an offering to God and God's visible acceptance of a past suffering shown now in Resurrection and triumph over death. The Eucharist is the sacrament of cosmic remembrance.

It is good to mention that the Christian remembrance or memorial is not simply a recalling to mind of an event which existed once upon a time. Recalling the mysteries or events of the life of Christ, who is risen, alive, always present, always active, is making them present in all their effectiveness and strength as when they were enacted by Christ. The proclamations of Christ, "This is my Body, This is my Blood," are as effective now in the memorial as when Christ pronounced them two thousand years ago. "Remembering, therefore, this precept of salvation, 'Do this in anamnesis, in remembrance of me'…' and everything that He has done for our sake, the Cross, the tomb, the Resurrection on the Third day, the Ascension into heaven, the enthronement at the right hand of the Father, the Second and glorious Coming again," are as many events happening in the now, and as real, true and effective as the words of consecration, "This is my Body, This is my Blood."

The whole Christ, in all his reality, offered on the Cross, is the Sacrifice. The whole reality of Christ's Sacrifice commemorated on the altar is the Sacrifice and the Meal. The Meal is not something that follows the sacrifice. Communion is the participation in the Sacrifice. The consecratory words recalling the mystery in its entire meaning provide the essential link between the commemorative Meal of the Church and the Sacrifice of Christ.

The breadth of perspective of the true meaning of God's intention and of his relation to creation is present here. The Father planned from all eternity and made this world and man and placed them in space and time. The Son embodied them in his own divine Person in the Incarnation and saved them by his offering, or sacrifice. The Holy Spirit renews this salvation and divinization by his descent at the Epiclesis, just as he did by his descent at Pentecost. All past divine historical facts become actual and alive before our very eyes. The world of faith takes shape, and the eternal mystery of God becomes reality in time.

PREPARATION

In order to be able to see the Invisible, to admire and burst into praise and thanks, one must first be attentive. The ministers, from the inside of the sanctuary, as well as the deacons on the outside, call for readiness and attention:

Let us stand well!

Let us stand in awe!

Let us be attentive!

Heaven and earth listen! God is pouring himself down upon us! We adore in a great hush. We plunge into the abyss of concentration and the rapture of a mystic vision. We shut out all noises. We collect ourselves and all our faculties to breathe praise and adore. The voices are hushed, and chanting ceases. The shortness of answers gives time to listen only. All attention is centered on the marvelous happening. (In the 14th and 15th centuries of Byzantine spiritual sloppiness, neglect and ignorance, the word "mystikos" before the prayers of the Anaphora started taking on the meaning of "silent," "secret." Thus the good news and the memory of God's goodness became "silent," and soon forgotten. Anaphora did not really mean much any more to the people except singing and dragging on an action that is by nature very solemn and very forceful. "Mystikos" does not mean "silent" or "secret." It means the deep warmth of meditation in a mystic vision.)

The athlete who prepares for a show, the poet who is caught by inspiration, the artist on the verge of performing, the saint at prayer, and the lover looking a the face of his beloved, are all on the alert. Artists and lovers, as well as saints, ready themselves in order to be awake, alive and attuned to vibrate to perfection and beauty. They are ready to live and communicate the God that is in them. They stand at attention. Indeed, they need to be "all together" for the moment of encounter. The past disturbs, the present scatters, the future entices. Artists and Saints open to the Beyond who is coming and is already here. As the orgasm of the bodily encounter has no meaning unless the two are present to each other, so prayer has no meaning unless we are present to God to listen and hear, to sing and play and breathe in harmony and unison with him.

As mentioned before, an ejaculation is a short, heartfelt prayer, an "arrow" that is hitting a target. An ejaculation is the cry of the poor, the one who is crushed by work and worries and is short of time. The rich man takes his time. He waits. For him, time and space are filled with the Holy Spirit. Time and space unite and do not separate. The Christian is rich. He waits. He stands at attention. He takes all the time he needs in order to be fully alive to himself and to his surroundings and to God. "Let us stand in awe!"

Conscious of what is to happen, the Christian realizes that he is not what he should be. "Awe" grips at his heart. Anxiety grips at the heart of any man who is to enter into a movement of life. The artist doubts. Was his preparation adequate? He wants to run back to his studio. The lover trembles. The vision of the poet blurs. The Saint vibrates. The Christian wonders: Am I ready?

Modern existentialists like Sartre, Camus and others call that moment of awe and anxiety "nausea." Eastern spiritual writers call it the "memory of death." The memory of death is not a morbid feeling of desperation like "nausea" is for modern existentialists. It is a flight into perfection, into God, who is the ultimate object of desire, and who inspires admiration and awe at his encounter. Awe is the very first condition and basic attitude for encountering the majesty of God.

This primary attitude of "anxiety" is also called the "prayer of attention." The prayer of attention is not a drug. It is a powerful movement of life which awakens to life and gives birth to life. It is amazement at the knowledge that another one exists. The consciousness of the existence of the "other" reveals the meaning of one's own existence. The Holy Spirit flings wide open the windows of consciousness, of the whole being, and makes it shake all over like he shook the upper room at Pentecost.

At this point, the amazement of the Christian seeks and strains to make others hear what he hears. He hears the remote and strange sound of angels singing: "Holy! Holy! Holy!" He sees the Holy Trinity at work, pouring down on him all the goodness and love that Infinity itself contains. He becomes a whirl of admiration and praise. He becomes "eucharistic."

Eucharist or thanksgiving is the expression of life in God and the only true relationship between man and God. It is what really "makes possible" all that will follow. The Christian bursts into thanks and praise:

It is fitting and right to sing to You, to bless You, to adore You, to give thanks to You, to glorify You who alone are truly God…How could anyone tell Your might and sing the praises You deserve, or describe all Your marvels in all places and times…O Master of all, You are eternal, invisible, beyond understanding, beyond description, the Father of Our Lord Jesus Christ, the Great God and Savior, the object of our hope…

Jesus Christ is the image of Your Goodness, the Seal who bears Your perfect likeness, revealing You his Father through Himself. He is the living Word, the true God, the Wisdom, the Life, the sanctification, the true Light…

By Him the Holy Spirit was made manifest, the Spirit of Truth, the Gift of adoption, the Foretaste of the future inheritance, the First fruit of eternal good, the Life Giving Power, the Fountain of sanctification. Empowered by Him, every rational and intelligent creature sings eternally to Your glory, for all are Your servants. It is You the angels, archangels, thrones, dominions praise and glorify…they cry one to the other with tireless voices and perpetual praise singing, proclaiming, shouting the hymn of victory and saying…Holy! Holy! Holy! Lord of Hosts. Heaven and earth are filled with your glory! Hosanna in the Highest.

I insist purposely on this divine and most mysterious part of the Christian religion. It is indeed of supreme importance. Once we have lost its meaning we lose the sense of joy and celebration that links us to God and to the salvation of Christ. The consequences of such a loss are incalculable for Christian life. If we are not impressed by the awesomeness of this action of our liturgy, if we are not imbued with its divine character, what else would have a real meaning in our Christian life? The only refuge would be rationalization, moralism, and all other anti-Gospel, non essentials like power, organization, worldly influence and triumphalism.

PRAISE

Christians are the associate of angels in their service before God. We enter into this association when we proclaim with them the holiness of the Trinity of God. At the beginning of every prayer we affirm this association when we recite the Trisagion:

"Holy is God," the Father who is origin, source and point of return of all creation. "Holy the Mighty," the Son. He is Mighty because he conquered evil and death and wrought salvation and resurrection. "He is Mighty because through Him the Father was revealed to us and the Holy Spirit came to this world" (Liturgy of Pentecost). "Holy the Immortal," the Holy Spirit who is life and life giving, whom nothing, no evil, no sin, no amount or gravity of sin can ever kill or wipe out from the soul of the Christian.

Once again Christians share in the life of angels and declare that we are sharing in their function and playing their role when the Lord is ready to enter the sanctuary in the offering of bread and wine! Christians declare with the whole congregation of the faithful: "We who mystically represent the Cherubim sing the thrice holy hymn: Holy! Holy! Holy!" Once again, at the Great Prayer of the Canon, we recognize that we are not only associates of the angels, but much more. We are even higher and more honorable than all the angels of heaven:

We thank you for this liturgy which you are pleased to accept from our hands, though there stand before you thousands of archangels and myriad of angels, Cherubim and Seraphim, six wings and many eyes…

As we surge on the wings of our dignity we join in the vision of Isaiah to sing the hymn of heaven: "Holy! Holy! Holy! Lord of Sabbaoth; Heaven and earth are filled with your glory. Hosanna in the highest!" The world to come is already here present in the "fullness of your glory." Christians reach the apex of their glory when they go beyond the horizon of the prophets and visionaries to look at the Trinity and melt into the divine Persons with an ineffable movement of joy. We address ourselves first to the Father:

Holy are You and all holy You and your only begotten Son and your Holy Spirit. Holy are you and all holy! Magnificent is your glory! You so loved your world as to give it your Son, That every one may have eternal life. The Son fulfilled your plan and your will on our behalf.

Then we recall the memory of the Son:

On the night Christ, the Son of God, was delivered up, rather He delivered Himself up for the life of the world, He took bread and looking at his disciples, apostles and all generations of the baptized He said: 'Take, eat: this is my body which is broken for you for the remission of sins.'

With the same simplicity and realism he took the cup of wine and said:

Take, drink of this all of you: This is my blood of the New Covenant. It will be shed for you and for all mankind for the remission of sins.

The majesty of the voice of Christ commands silence! Heaven and earth cheered it. Amen!

WHAT A SURPRISE! AMEN!

Human ears seek and strain to know if the angels and the clouds of heavenly witnesses heard the strange declaration. The same voice that spoke the words, "Let there be light," has just spoken again: "This is my Body! This is my Blood!" It is, indeed! It is! And the universe trembles! The vibrations of the words of Christ caress our faces, our hair, our very clothes, our hands and every part of our body. Our ears carry his voice to the inner depth of our being. The impossible becomes real and the unhoped for becomes a fact. The feeling is awe and recognition.

We recognize not only the fact that bread and wine are now the Body and Blood of Christ, but all the other marvelous deeds of God for us are as real and as present. For us men and for our salvation "he accepted the cross and the tomb." For us "he rose on the third day." For us "he ascended into heaven and sat us at the right hand of the Father." For us "he will come again in glory." This is the Anamnesis, the Memorial, which makes present the divine events of the life of Christ and which we, in fact, make manifest here and now.

The truth of Christ is not in the intellect or in the brain only; it penetrates the whole person. It is in our whole being and all around us. Like the universe that accepted the first explosion of light without a question, the Christian accepts this truth and does not seek explanation. We do not need any explanation. Only the blind asks about light, about the sunshine, about beauty and colors.

Saint Gregory of Nyssa sees in Abraham the image of the Christian who does not ask questions about the tremendous miracles of God.

Men who do not believe pose questions. They ask for signs or proofs. But the Christian sees in "proofs" wounds in the truth of the Lord and the Lord refuses them. Silence is one of the qualities of God. Any proof that imposes itself on man's will violates his conscience. That is why God speaks facts and hides his omnipotence behind his silence. He has spoken through the Prophets. He has spoken during his life on earth. He has spoken at Pentecost. And now, says Nicolas Cabasilas, "it is in silence that God declares his tremendous love for man and his incomprehensible respect before Man's freedom…" "The hands of the Crucified Christ cover our eyes but they are pierced hands, and our eyes can see through them" (Quoted by Evdokimov). We hear the declaration of the Lord over the bread that it is his Body, over the wine that it is his Blood, and we proclaim our consent to his truthfulness: Amen!

The truth of Christ is clear, alive and inspires visions. The Christian has the eyes of the angels, the eyes of God, the real eyes of man, which sees the essence of things. After having heard the voice of the Lord declaring the bread to be his Body, and the wine to be his Blood, the Christian never asks "how." It is simply the Body and Blood, the real and total Christ, just as when he walked around the lake and as he is now in his Resurrection. The Christian has the mystical knowledge and a paradoxical grasp of the Inconceivable. In an intuitive, primordial and simple approach he knows beyond the process of the intellect. The Fathers say that the Christian "hopes for what exists already," and remembers what is to come in the immediate, "because he drinks at the source of the living water."

It is indeed a tremendous miracle to see God taking flesh and becoming man, and a greater miracle still to see Him suspended on the cross. But the highest and sum of all miracles is your ineffable presence under the appearance of bread and wine, O Christ! Truly You did institute, through this sacrament, a remembrance of all Your marvels. How merciful of You, O God, to give Yourself as food to those who stand in awe before You,…to recall your Covenant forever, and to remember your passion and Your death until the day of your glorious coming (403).

RETURN TO THE FATHER

The ministers around the altar and the assembly of the baptized are now all wrapped in adoration. The minister celebrant crosses his hands on the altar, the right hand stretching over the left hand, to take up the paten which lays on his left, the left hand stretching over the right hand to take up the chalice which is at the right side. He elevates both Body and Blood in a gesture toward the East, then toward the West, then to the North and to the South, thus planting Christ in the four corners of the universe, or rather gathering the universe, or rather gathering the universe in these four movements to offer it in Christ and with Christ to the Father, saying:

We offer You Your own
from what is Your own
for all and for the sake of all,

In the Roman liturgy, this same intention is expressed by the words, "In him, with him, through him."

This is "Eucharist," real life, a movement of love and adoration towards God. To offer is to thank and to enter into communion with God. In Christ, who is the perfect Eucharist, we become "eucharistic." In him, God becomes our life, "to take in our hands the whole world as if it were an apple" and offer it to God. This is our Eucharist, our Sacrifice also. Christ performed the Eucharist once and for all. We do it in our turn in Christa and in remembrance of Christ. In this offering all things have reached their end and their destiny.

What a simplicity in the grandeur and nobility of this gesture! The whole history of salvation, the whole revelation of God's love, the whole meaning of Christianity is here made manifest. The whole value and the very meaning of life is given to the Father. The Father recognizes the whole creation in his Son and pours upon the whole universe the same love he has for his Son. "In this offering," says Cyril of Jerusalem, "we bring to the presence of God the Father heaven, earth, oceans, sun, moon and the entire creation…," and we break out in praise and thanks:

We praise You. We bless You. We give thanks to You, O Our God.

We become ourselves a hymn of glorification:
All that is
What speaks and what is silent
All declare You.

All that is,
What thinks and what cannot think
All praise You.

The world desire, the world sighing,
Moves towards You.
Your world sends up to You
A hymn of silence! (*Face of God*, p. 31).

THE HOLY SPIRIT

By contacting this sublime reality of the return of creation to its source and origin, the Father, we encounter the world of the soul, of the Spirit, of our instincts, of our intuitions. We encounter the values proper to interiority which are completely different from subjectivity. Interiority puts us in contact with the source of our being. We become spiritual, not dreamers, but people of depth. We live with the Holy Spirit.

Until now we have marveled at the works of God and praised him for his deeds of salvation. The Father "out of nothing brought us into being, and when we had fallen he raised us up again…" The Son declared matter to be his Body and Blood and suffered and died and rose to make us one with him. Now we fall on our knees, begging for the descent of the Holy Spirit: "We ask, we pray and entreat: Send down Your Holy Spirit upon us and upon these gifts here offered."

It is another awesome and most astounding action of God for us. The Holy Spirit comes to fill us and to fill the oblations of bread and wine with his own eternal Being and Presence by acting personally and creatively. Bread and wine and the baptized receive him and are possessed by him. The Wonderful event of Pentecost is now renewed and is indeed most real! "Our God who loves mankind, having received these gifts on his holy altar in heaven, he sends down upon us his Divine Grace and the Holy Spirit…"

Now, anyone partaking of this Bread and Wine will receive the fullness of the Holy Spirit who is "cleansing of the soul, remission sins." The Body and Blood of Christ will confer also "the communion, the fellowship" of the one ness with the Holy Spirit himself who becomes also "fullness of the Kingdom of heaven, intimate confidence in the Father," who sees only his Son present and who will not "judge juridically or condemn," but save. The Spirit of God "becomes closer to me than my own breath" (Gregory of Nazianzus), and "more intimate than my own intimacy" (Augustine). By this descent of the Holy Spirit upon the bread and wine anyone eating the Body or drinking the Blood of Christ receives the divine uncreated energies in all their holiness and majesty. Sins are forgiven and life is given Father, Son, and Holy Spirit, the Trinity takes hold of us and divinizes us. Theosis is realized!

Ministers at the altar and all the assembly of worshipers fall down on their faces saying: Amen! Amen! Amen!

Christians are eucharistic. We conclude all the prayers and all the marvelous remembrances of the deeds and love of God by this final proclamation "And grant that with one mouth and one heart, we may glorify and extol your most noble and magnificent name, O Father, Son, and Holy Spirit."

The rest is silence!

CHAPTER 14

THE COMMUNITY

The joy, peace and certainty that celebration creates have the natural tendency to be contagious. They belong to the community. Community is the place where the celebration witnesses to God in his works, and where it teaches humanity that God cares, and that he is true and real. It teaches also the meaning of his presence and of his living, dynamic action in the world.

The ancients called this gathering of the faithful "Synax," a convention, a community that looks to eternity, a solemn and joyous family togetherness where the members of the same family take part in an action of life.

Being together in community, the faithful experience more readily both their unity in Christ and the power of the Spirit. Angels and Saints are only a part of this community. They all look up to God. They embrace the today of God and welcome the tomorrow of the Kingdom where all the horizons of yesterday disappear in the mist of the past.

What goes on in the assembly, or community, is the living together of an event of life. When people are together they become a living event. The multitudes are at an incessant work of creation, the creation of an ever new humanity, always flowing, never fixed. Christ himself liked crowds and assemblies, the only place where celebration is contagious.

God, people, creation, Christ and his entire life are the motives and subjects for wonder and joy that enable us to enter into the Kingdom. God, people, creation, each is a poem and a miracle of beauty that makes us sing in glory, awe and joy. Each is a celebration designed to make our life a celebration, and the community the ground of celebration. An ennobling movie, a theater play, an artistic performance are also part of the "Kingdom" of Christ.

Christians meet for divine celebration in order to make more meaningful, and to implant in the heart of people, what is already charged with light, hope and radiance. In their assembly, the Christians remember and proclaim to the world an event or an action of God in which they find their own glory, their inner beauty and personal dignity. Even when they recognize and proclaim their sinfulness, it is to proclaim much louder the goodness and generosity of God's forgiveness.

Christian celebration consists essentially in providing elements of education to people for their spiritual as well as human interests, and for the experience of the presence of God acting among them. We deserve to enter into such intimate realities of life and to encounter their inner and outer meaning and beauty and thus be filled with joy and hope.

Experience is a mode of speaking about God and his mysteries which illumines and harmonizes all of our human irregularities and heals our human wounds. The experience of God softens our crushed hearts and enables them to receive the story of the wonders of God. Celebration helps us to see an action of life in which we take part. We are present at a spectacle, as it were, at the very time of the event which is always here present with us:

> Behold, our redemption is now manifest,
> for God is ineffably joined to mankind…
> The Virgin has accepted the joyful news,
> the earth has become heaven,
> And the world has been turned into paradise.
> Let the whole creation rejoice
> And sing a hymn of praise:
> O Lord, our Maker and our Redeemer,
> glory to You.

MEMORIAL

For the Christian, a past event is a remembrance which is a present feast. The remembrance is both a memory of an event and a prophetic vision of the future. The Christian turns towards the past, which is his foundation, and towards the future, which is his purpose. He rests on the past and looks towards eternity. This is the religious experience of the feast. Action and performance are so illuminating and so convincingly true that all those near and far who hear them or see them would stand and say: "Surely Christ is the Truth and he is the Sun of our searching."

Past and future are somehow present. The events are the work of

God in whom there is no time. In the Christian feast, time ceases to exist. It is a present experience. The redemptive work of Christ takes up everything into the now and extends it to eternity. The commemoration of the wondrous works of God becomes an announcement of salvation. We never cease repeating that "Today is the Day…" "Today" will extend to tomorrow, to all times, to eternity.

Today is the Day of the Resurrection: O Nations, let us be jubilant, for this Passover is the Passover of the Lord, in that Christ our God made us pass from death to life and from earth to heaven.

The Church is called, it is her mission, to fill every person with the joy and the hope and the deep reality of love and life that are in Christ.

All actions and performances in the Church are communal. It is the community which is present and which celebrates and proclaims its God and Savior. Individuals are not neglected, however. They sway with their bodies, move their hands, raise and lower their eyes, bow their heads. They recite the prayers, loudly and clearly. Their voices rise and fall in heartfelt supplication. When suddenly a silence is commanded, all becomes aware of each other's presence. They exchange, in silence, their hope and aspiration. Their gathering in community becomes more solemn and deeply serious in an atmosphere of invisible beauty:

> Today the Virgin is on her way to the cave
> Where she will give birth in a manner beyond understanding
> To the Word who is from all eternity…
> Rejoice, therefore, O Universe!
> And with the angels and the Shepherds
> Glorify the One who of his own free will
> Appeared on earth a new born babe
> But He is at the same time God from all Eternity!

Christians do not come together to listen to theoretical explanations whether they be "infallible" definitions or interpretations put forward for the sake of intellectual knowledge. They come together to be possessed by the awesome Truth himself.

In every assembly where people gather to celebrate, no one is a spectator or a pupil. Every one is engaged in an action. Every one is in "readiness," calling on and waiting for the coming of the Lord, "who is coming" yet always present. They gather to receive the saving power of God and rejoice in his goodness and glory. They do not assemble to learn morality, commandments or good behavior. The Christian assembly is that good, generous humus where people are nourished and transformed. The only morality we should learn in the Church is the morality of how to eliminate the obstacles to growth and to the free flowing of the sap of life which springs from the Holy Spirit of God. We learn how to open and abandon ourselves to the revelation of God, to experience him, and thus be able to witness to our religious experience.

By its contact with the Christian celebration, the world will experience that Christ is real, that he is really present, and that he is the object of its aspirations: "Explain it we cannot," reported the messengers of the pagans when they returned to Russia from Constantinople, "but we certainly realized that heaven was on earth." This is the Memorial of Christ in the Christian assembly.

OBJECTIVITY

The Christian celebration, like any other artistic celebration, is primarily to be proclaimed to the community by an individual. It is devised to be presented on a stage by actors whose performance will bring every member of the community, even those who do not comprehend the words, into the mystery of God. It takes hold of every spectator and creates in them awe and recognition. The presence of the Spirit makes the divine event present in the here and now and changes the soul with a high emotional quality which becomes a real dynamism in the soul. If Christians, for some reason, happen to fall away from prayer and the Feast, the dynamism they have acquired in the celebration is never lost. It remains dormant in the subconscious mind. But when the grace of God touches it again it is activated and energized and it bursts into the sphere of consciousness with a tremendous force of delight and inner joy.

What happens, really, in the Christian celebration, and what is so very important, is that heaven and earth join in a dance of triumph. In Christ, death becomes life. Hades is no more. And life is in every one. When they really celebrate, Christians feel changed. They are made one with Christ and one with all others. All the members of the Christian community are welded together in a shared triumph, and they communicate to each other and witness to the world, not what they think or feel, but what they have become.

There is an intellectual content to every Christian celebration. In the course of the celebration, a vital communication and understanding pass from person to person, group to group. The Church believes that every Christian should be a theologian. A theologian is someone who has experienced God, who can talk to God, and who can communicate something of his experience to others. The celebration in the Church is the ground, the generous humus, which permits people to grow, admire and praise God and the goodness of his actions.

One of the main characteristics of Christianity and of Christian celebration is objectivity. Christians admire God in the glory of his Majesty, clothed with his attributes. We are participants overwhelmed by the generosity of such a God. God is therefore held up for the worship and adoration of his people. Christ, in his Person and work, is set before the mind in a most realistic manner. We consider his birth and all events that accompanied it; his life; the words he spoke; the work he did; his passion and all its agony; the denial of Peter; the remorse of Judas; the Crucifixion; the darkness, the terror, the opened graves; the penitent thief; the loud cry, the death all are expressed in Church hymnography in plain, unmistakable language. Christian hymnography is indeed a pictorial representation of the history of Redemption, which by engaging the mind appeals ultimately to the heart and its emotions. Here we see and experience that Redemption and all the deeds of God are really "for us men and for our salvation."

LITURGY

In Ancient Greece celebration was called "leitourgia," a public service or artistic performance carried out for the benefit of the community. The great works of playwrights, like Sophocles and Euripedes, were considered to be of both a civil and religious nature and importance. These works of arts, as every form of art, were aimed at creating in people good taste and enjoyment of life. Our artistic productions of today movies, television, theatre and the like are of the same type and nature. They are works of art in which life, or a certain aspect of life, is enacted to inspire, instruct, and ultimately, to deepen the realization of the awesomeness of the work of God in his creation. Each aspect of creation is a "leitourgia," a celebration where we exercise our universal priesthood.

The task of financing and staging these dramas was, in olden times, entrusted to an honorable and responsible citizen whose contribution to the public was considered also to be his "leitourgia," his service rendered to the community. The production of these artistic works was given to actors and artists whose dedication and self-sacrifice created in people a facility to understand and enjoy life and maintain it in good order. Acting was also a liturgy.

Christianity used the word "leitourgia," first, for any public office, or ministration. The Apostle Paul used it for the ministration of charity. Ecclesiastical writers applied it both to civil and sacred functions, to the function of a magistrate or of a bishop.

Later the adjective "mystical" was added to mean the renewal of the sacrifice of the Lord Jesus Christ on the altar. Still later, the words "Hiera," "hierurgia" and "Thysia" were used in the same meaning. These words generally signified the performance of the great prayer of Christ and his sacrifice offered to God for the salvation of the world. The liturgy of Christ takes place first and foremost in his own personal worship of the Father, begun on earth in his Incarnation, and continuing now in heaven and enduring forever in his Risen Person. It is this very same worship that is renewed and re enacted on our altars. It is called the "Holy and Divine Liturgy."

Since Christians are baptized in Christ, we share in the worship of Christ and in his glorification of the Father, and in the sanctification of the world. The same word, "Liturgia," came also to indicate the act of solemn corporate worship and prayers offered to God by the priestly society of Christians.

In the Antiphons, for instance Christians witness to the goodness of the Lord and shout their own hopes and joys at the sight of Christ's action of salvation. Historically speaking, the Antiphons were popular demonstrations and processions through the streets and winding roads of a given locality, from church to church, leading to the main Church were celebration had to take place. These processions were meant to gather on their way the "good and the sinners, inviting every one, believer and unbeliever to the wedding feast of the King" (Matt. 22:8).

The word "Antiphon" means a refrain of a reading or of a rhetorical declamation often repeated during the course of a procession. Antiphons are devised to provoke in people enthusiasm and joy and help them see the goodness of God who hears the immense desire of humanity. Humanity sighs and longs for the coming of the Savior, and God bends towards the earth, sending his Son to be incarnate. Salvation is then seen as present and already working among us. These street demonstrations, as they are worked out in the Antiphons, end in a peaceful and nerve relaxing hymn which sings the presence of the Son among men:

O Only Begotten Son and Word of God,
You are Immortal God!
For our Salvation
You condescended to take flesh in the Virgin Mary.
You became Man.
You were crucified.
And by your death you crushed death
You are real God, One with the Father and the Holy Spirit.

Once we have seen that the promises of God and the expectations of his people have been fulfilled, we understand that the "wedding feast" is open to all and in full progress. And excited stir runs through the congregation: the Bridegroom is now coming! We prepare to receive him. The ministers form a great procession with lighted candles, covered with a cloud of incense. The bejeweled Holy Gospel Book, which is the symbol and sign of Jesus Christ himself, is carried high on the head of the celebrant, or the deacon. The whole assembly rises to honor the coming of the Lord, using singing, imagination and all the human emotions. Everyone bows profoundly at the passage of Christ, adoring him really present in his book of life. By bowing and by many signs of the Cross, everyone proclaims his or her readiness to hear his voice and heed the lessons of his love.

The Gospel book is thus brought with solemnity and majesty into the midst of the congregation and finally to the sanctuary. It is this type of dramatic demonstration that appeals to our modern television and radios, but we should not expose to uninitiated eyes and ears the most holy and most intimate part of Christ's Sacrifice, the Anaphora or Canon of the Holy and Divine Liturgy. The Consecration of bread and wine on radio or television is a desecration of holy things.

After the entrance of the Gospel Book and its enthronement on the altar, the throne of God as it were, the people go on with their merry celebration of the Saints or of an event in the life of Christ, remembering again a phase of the deeds and goodness of God. Christians assemble to celebrate the saints also. Heroes and benefactors of humanity, the saints have surrendered themselves to God and to their brothers and sisters. They became pure transparencies for God's action, and thus they are to us extended radiances of the Incarnation.

In each and every celebration we find the full theological meaning of events and mysteries explained in simple words full of warmth and exuberance, often deeply poetical, the exuberance of a poet, and the buoy-ant beauty of life. Abstraction and abstract expressions have their place in schools and monastery study periods. Poetry, exuberance and music are for meetings. They are the privilege of people gathering in joy, in life, and in the knowledge of their transformation into the Divine. The Church unfolds the essential movements of the revelation of God to man in a joyous, dramatic and perfumed atmosphere of celebration.

The sacramental prayer of the Holy and Divine Liturgy, for instance, begins with the humble listening of every person, then proceeds to the welcoming of Christ in his Gospel; then to oblation, intercession, ado-ration, consecration; finally, it culminates, for the benefit of the baptized only, into transformation into Christ through the contact with him in consecration and in Communion. In each and every performance of the sacraments, we find theology explained in poetical words. And all the mysteries are expressed in a radiant setting. They are celebrations of God and of his dialogue with us; celebrations of mankind and of our common destiny.

THE LEADER OF THE CELEBRATION

A spiritual man is essentially dependent on his senses and on his body to make contact with things beyond himself. He lives and moves most vividly in signs and symbols that point to a deeper reality, and ulti-mately to the reality of God. By words, gestures, literary and artistic means, he draws ever nearer to a world richer and wider than all mate-rial realities. Ceremonies and celebrations are necessary to express his consciousness and to allow him to transcend the immediate and con-crete in order to reach inner realities. Ceremonies and celebrations are necessary to express also the response of the soul to the goodness and mercy of God.

The Church is not a society assembled around a program or around a morality to be handed down. The Church is the people who believe in Jesus Christ and who assemble around him. It is Jesus Christ who assembles. It is he who calls the Church and makes her a reality. He gives her life and meaning.

The bishop is the sign and symbol of Jesus Christ in the assembly of the Church. He determines ceremonies and celebrations and is the exemplary performer and leader. The bishop has always been consid-ered the essential person in the functioning of the assemblies of

Christians. He will always be essential and there will be no eucharistic Church on earth without the bishop. His mission is to manifest that it is Jesus Christ who is at the source of the life of the Church. He witnesses to the universality of Christ by presenting to the world the pains, hopes, difficulties and joys of a particular locality where Christians assemble and meet. He witnesses that the faith of his local Church and of the Christians of his time is the very same faith as the faith of the Apostles, and that it is just as strong. He consecrates bread and wine and presides at the Eucharist. He is the sign of unity of Christians because he is chosen from the community and by the community for the service of the community.

In the Church there is also the priest. The priest is sent by the bishop whose helper he is. In the community of the Church, ordination of a priest by the bishop is not a contract, but a consecration and dedication of a man to a special mission. The mission of the priest is to be the collaborator of his bishop. Even when the community elects the priest, it is the bishop who ordains him.

The celebration of ordination is not a celebration in honor of the priest's generosity or dedication. It is rather the celebration of the Christian community who express thanks to God for his generosity to his people and to his Church by offering the gift of his life and of his care through the priest. Those who are perplexed and worried about the year 2,000 A.D. should rejoice in the fact that as there were bishops and priests for the past two thousand years, there will always be bishops and priests from one state of social life or another, for all ages, until the consummation of the world.

Because the bishop and his priests represent Christ and are the servants of their people, they enjoy a certain freedom in conducting their religious services. There should be no rigid legalism to stifle or blind their vision and inspiration. The Church has always showed a concern to adapt the liturgy to the circumstances of life:

Like the concentric rings of growth of an ancient tree, they are a compendium and faithful mirror of the millennial life of the Church, presenting to us not only the ancient and lovely rite of the patristic age, but the more splendid development of the mighty Byzantine empire, the overcharged taste of the eighteenth century, of false classicism and the baroque, as well as the reign of the present mechanical and industrial age. A refined taste may deplore the lack of restraint in many of the adjuncts of modern Byzantine worship, but a sounder Christian sense is constrained to admit a persisting and robust consonance with the desires of the common people, whose church it is, rather than with that of a clique of eccentric clergy or theory ridden archeologists (Oakley, The Orthodox Liturgy).

But as in the enjoyment of every freedom, there is danger. Now there exists an accumulation of usages which have no more significance or meaning. There are also truncations and adaptations which are out of place. Freedom and liberty led by a dignified and artistic inspiration can always remedy these complications of texts and the lack of taste and harmony.

Rules and rubrics are necessary, and bishops and priests know them and carefully study the. Rules and regulations are the general structure of the life of the whole Church expressed according to a certain pattern and theological understanding. They are to be respected and obeyed. Nevertheless, what is accomplished in the celebrations of the Church has to have significance for all the people of God according to their mentality and conditions of life. We might say that the celebration of the Church is the experience of all, offered to all, to be relived by all, always according to the need and the circumstances of life and work of the people of God.

Celebrations are designed for people and performed with people. They generally dramatize the meaning of the events of the life of Christ or of the presence of God in the world. In these public functions there is constant motion and personal participation. The bishop or the priest celebrants do not assume all the roles of the celebration. They have the "leading role." They are the actors who breathe life and meaning and inspire everyone around them to understand the meaning of the actions and his or her own dignity. They share their role with the deacons and the assembly.

The priests do not say at the altar. They, and their retinue of assistants, come out of the sanctuary and walk in the midst of the congregation, first, perhaps, to incense, then to carry the Gospel book; finally to transfer the oblations or to receive them in a solemn procession where angels mingle with us to carry the King of all and welcome his coming among them. They go around the church to sprinkle people with perfume, to shower the congregation now with flowers, now with a smile, and yet another time with encouragement and a blessing.

The bishop, or his assistant the priest, is leader of the assembly of Christians. He is a doer of life, therefore not a "rubricist." He believes that there is a fuller dimension to reality and relationships than meets the eye. His function is to celebrate and proclaim not only in word, but also and especially in deed, the experience that fills him with conviction and joy. With the eyes of his mind and heart he sees the beauty of the message and the possibilities for its symbolic bodily articulation and word enunciation, in order to reveal the self and the truth of God.

The bishop in his religious function, or his assistant the priest, says much more than anyone can understand. They are on a deep level of maturity and ecstasy, recreating the love act of Christ. Their faith is an ocean of love which moves them to find the wave that their listeners will catch and ride. They move them to the same intensity of love that is in them, strengthen their inner dispositions, lift them up into what they have acquired in private prayer, and of personal experience of God.

If these ministers are penetrated by conviction they will become more fervent and impressive: they will be eloquent. But if, unfortunately, they do not find the flame, they will sound and look empty and fake. Their posture, their walk, and their whole bearing speak of dignity and purpose. They are not conducting simply a "beautiful," "colorful," and "interesting ceremony." In fact, they are engaged in an awesome and terribly "serious action." They put man face to face with his Creator, Savior and God as they themselves have seen him in their private lives and meditations and prayers.

Renewal is the fruit of the Spirit who is gentleness, purity, deep artistic taste, and openness. Renewal has nothing in common with the hooting bad taste of the divinely disobedient, or the tasteless newness of invented "underground liturgies." It has no share either in the abstract words and stilted gestures of the bored and tired. Psalmody, reading of Scriptures, processions, sermons, and every movement of the bishop and of the priest, are many feasts of glory. They are designed to glorify God and give us the real meaning of our dignity and destiny. Believers and unbelievers, Jews and baptized, are welcome to come to these ceremonies and to participate in them. The bishop, priest and their Christian assemblies wish to invite every human person to their banquet of joy and dignity, and to be guests and participants. All the earth is called upon to share in such a living movement of life and love.

A Christian feast should be broadcast by radio, television, and movies, publicized by the press. It should spread from person to person to convey the real sense of renewal and hope. The fourth Council of Carthage in the fourth century had a rule "that the bishop shall not prohibit anyone to enter the church and hear the word of celebration and the announcement of God whether he be gentile, Jew or heretic, till the Service of Catechumens was ended." (Notice that these same people cannot be admitted to the Holy Eucharist.) This rule was honored in East and West alike. In many of his homilies, St. John Chrysostom speaks not only of Catechumens being present at his sermons but also of heretics and pagans and Jews. In his homily on Psalm 44, he wishes that more Jews and more heretics and heathens were present to hear him explain the prophetic meaning of that psalm.

But there is a special mystery, deep and incomprehensible, that should never be exposed to uninitiated eyes the mystery of the consecration of the Body and Blood of Christ. One must have the eyes of God, the eyes of angels, and the gift of the Spirit, the very special eyes of the initiated baptized, to see an invisible reality and to confess and comprehend the incomprehensible. The fact of bread and wine becoming the Body and Blood of Christ our Lord, our God and Savior, cannot be appreciated and adored except by the elect of God, those who are possessed by the flame of the Spirit.

When our modern television presents to the eyes of indiscriminate people "bread" and "wine" "this is the Lamb of God," "this is my body," "this is my blood" there is desecration and scandal! We Christians owe a special respect and consideration to all men, and especially to the eyes and ears of those who trust us and who want to trust our credibility. The Holy and divine consecration, and the most intimate or "revealed" action of Holy Communion, should never be surrendered to "enemies," which means those who are not able to understand, and whose natural reaction will be scorn, disbelief and ridicule.

Our Christian truth is meant to live, not merely survive. It has to develop and grow, while remaining in a profound Christian sense, the same. Christianity triumphs not in hiding, but when it faces reality and challenge. With very little effort and even less imagination, what used to be called "the Liturgy of the Catechumens" could be restored to its original meaningfulness as a function of the pastoral mission of the Church who is called to "evangelize" the baptized and the unbaptized, the believer and unbeliever.

There is much to learn from the Chronicles of Nestor concerning the envoys of Vladimir, Prince of Kiev (978-1015), who sent his messengers to various countries in search of the true religion. (I briefly mentioned this incident before.) They went first to the Mohammedans of Bulgaria: "There is no joy in their prayer," they reported to Vladimir, "and therefore their system cannot be good." Traveling next to Germany and Rome they found the worship of the Romans more satisfactory, but complained that "there, too, religion was without life and without beauty." Finally they journeyed to Constantinople and there at last, as they attended some celebrations in the Church of Holy Wisdom, they discovered what they desired: "We did not know if we were on earth or in heaven! For there is no such splendor to be found anywhere on earth describe it we cannot! We know only that it is there that God dwells among men."

When the celebration of the feast incorporates the patterns and habits of a culture and national way of life, and is shaped by these patterns and habits, it becomes a way of expressing "one's self." Worship becomes something in which man is lifted up above peculiarities and even local differences to participate in the on going heavenly worship of Christ himself. It is in and through this worship that we can transcend our national differences and be united with one another. The basic pattern of our worship which unifies us, will, of course, be governed by the life and pattern of Christ himself, for then it is in his name and not in our own that we will worship the Father. The worship will not be a way of expressing only ourselves, but away in which Christ confesses us before the Father through our love and unity and respect of others.

Because celebrations are popular, the Church becomes naturally the Church of the people. It becomes even more precious than one's own home. All the celebrations of the mysteries of heaven take on a special quality of joy and beauty in which one longs to participate. Because the liturgy is so interwoven with daily life, the Church becomes the common possession and the pride of the people .The Christian faith becomes the bond which in large measure takes the place of a nationality.

Persecution, oppression, famine, or the call for better social opportunities drove Christian peoples away from their countries of Europe and the East to settle in the New World. But in their voluntary exile they remembered their Church with its ceremonies and its songs. Before securing their own livelihood and organizing their social life, they set out to organize their churches "as in the old country," with their own priests and their own customs, so that they might worship and serve God in the way in which their traditions had taught them. Misunderstanding, opposition, and seemingly insurmountable difficulties were in their path. They were persecuted. But their courage and their faith endured all kinds of sacrifices, until their dreams were realized and each one had his own church. Such a phenomenon is possible only when religion is a real way of life: popular.

When we stop living the truth of the Gospel we insist on intellectualizing it, thus forging a religion of words and concepts. We neglect the Spirit and the heart and develop theories and formulae which shut out Jesus and impose a Christ without humanity. Men then incarnate Christ in officials, administrators, inquisitors, judges, and rulers. The Holy Spirit today is shaking our intellectualism and the barriers we have been building around Christ and around God. Our modern world is hungry and looking for the day when the Church and her ceremonies and celebrations are given back to the people in freedom and in beauty.

It is not possible to understand Christianity by only reading or talking about it. It is necessary to experiences its life, its actuality, be being present at its celebrations: "Come and see!" The organic and completely self evident center of Christianity is in its celebrations.

CHAPTER 15

THE TRANSFIGURED CHRISTIAN

Now the Christian is on the way to the glory of the kingdom, to the plenitude of the Feast, and to perfect celebration. The mystical chamber of the Bridegroom is ready and vibrant with expectation. Here is the end of all processions, the oasis of the journey and its fulfillment. Having been immersed in the Godhead and transformed by grace into what God is by nature, the Christian is on the point of being transfigured and becoming a flame of divinity. Christ is now going to mingle his Body and Blood and his divine personality with the Christian's body and blood and human personality.

After the Consecration and Epiclesis there is the meal, the communion with the Body and Blood of Christ. The Eucharist is indeed, with the Incarnation, the most hidden and yet more glorious reality of God identifying himself with his creature in a supreme act of surrender. In creation, God visited nothingness and transformed it into an existing reality. In the Incarnation, he assumed humanity and united it to himself. In Holy Communion, he identifies it with himself and gives the communicant the capacity to become a divine reality.

Communion takes place not only in the action of the actual eating and drinking but also in the whole eucharistic prayer which preceded it. Communion includes both Consecration and Epiclesis. The Consecration declared the elements of bread and wine to be the Body and Blood of Christ. It divinized them and brought them back to their Source and Author, the Father. Epiclesis filled them with the Holy Spirit who by his descent transformed them into life giving elements, carriers of the life of the Trinity, "so that to those who partake of them, they may be for the cleansing of the soul, for the remission of sins, for the fellowship of the Holy Spirit" (285). Communion is, therefore, part of the Sacrificial ritual, not separate from it.

The command of the Lord at the time of consecration was clear and imperative: "Take, eat, all of you…," and "drink of this all of you…" When the Christian obeys the command and eats and drinks "of this my body and this my blood," he enters most closely into Christ's sacrifice. Christ acts upon him sacramentally to draw him into his sacrificial offering and to sweep him up into the loving oblation by which He offered himself to the Father. Communion brings the holy elements forward to proclaim and accomplish their sacred meaning. For this reason they are called "sacred gifts," "awesome mysteries," or "life giving mysteries."

Communion is the supreme reality of the love that overflows from God to intensify in his creature the expression of his glory. Here and made physically present all the Covenants or Alliances of God from the very beginning of creation, through Adam, the first man, to Noah, to Abraham, to Moses and to the Lord Jesus Christ. The Kingdom of God and the Redemption God planned from all eternity are now made real and vibrant where man can see both himself and God in a new light.

Communion and the whole eucharistic prayer that preceded it are called "the Sacrifice of Christ." The concept of sacrifice is borrowed from the Jewish religion of which Christianity is the extension and perfection. Sacrifice was, in the Old Testament, divinely ordained as a means of approaching God; the means of grace and salvation whereby the Covenant relationship of Israel with Yahweh was maintained and strengthened. As sacraments of the Covenant, sacrifices made possible the realization of this fellowship.

Biblical scholars tell us that "whether the sacrifice was offered publicly or privately, for the individual or a group, whether it was the appointed rite for the Sabbath or New Moon, Feast day or Passover, it was always a sacramental realization of God's Covenant" (S. Whale). Sacrifice was also for the expiation of sin, the effecting of atonement, and the removal of sin. In the sacrifice there was always a sense in which man, in offering, offered himself. But its blood symbol, say biblical scholars, suggested the offering of a man's life as the basis of his fellowship with God.

Animal sacrifice is no longer offered by Jews. We Christians regard it as having been superseded by the offering and death of Christ on the Cross. The principle underlying sacrifice is that blood is the seat and seed of life, the carrier of life. When therefore blood was sprinkled on humans in the Old Testament, it gave new life to those it touched. When the Blood of Christ was sprinkled from the cross, It gave new life to the whole world. The whole world is bathed in the life of Christ.

The essential nature of sacrifice resides in an expiatory gift to God and a communion meal, an act of social fellowship in which God and his worshipers unite by partaking together of the Flesh and Blood of the sacred Victim. All these elements of Old Sacrifice are supremely and gloriously actualized in all their fullness in the Eucharist of the Christian.

The encounter and bodily embrace with Christ awakens in the communicant awareness of what he really is in himself and by himself. He is a sinner. The Communicant sees in a clear vision all the imperfections, failures and stumblings of his daily life. He has broken the commandments. He has splattered the beauty of the divine image in him. He experiences an overwhelming sense of sorrow and loving fear: "I have sinned, O Lord, I have sinned before your face, and I am not worthy to lift up my eyes to your glory. I have provoked your goodness; I have transgressed your commandments and disobeyed your statutes…"

But Christianity is not a subjective relation to God. It is an objective movement. It is a life which has meaning and substance only in Christ. It is Christ who gives, Christ who loves, and Christ God who sanctifies and saves. Man can lose many battles, even all the battles of life, but Christ is the final Victory and Resurrection. The outcome of life in Christ is a banquet and a kingdom and a supreme triumph. The prayers of the Church are insistent in their assertion that "The bread and wine will be for the healing of my soul and body, for the enlightenment of my mind and the protection of my life. They give me confidence in You…"

If there is a sorrow in the heart of the Christian for the many misdeeds of his life, it is a sorrow in which a new upsurge of love restores the joy of living. Sorrow is never hopeless, never final, never inspires guilt. It is an irresistible urge to carry on and begin a new song. Here again the ancient prayers of Christians strongly affirmed this fact: "When I receive my share of your holy gifts I am united to your Body and Blood, O Lord. May I have you to abide in me with the Father and the Holy Spirit. Grant me, until my last breath, to receive the Bread and the Wine which are your Body and Blood, and thereby to receive fellowship with the Holy Spirit as a provision for the journey to eternal life, and as an acceptable answer at your dread judgment seat!"

And again, Saint John Damascus declares what countless generations of Christians have been repeating for more than a thousand years:

"O Lord and Master Jesus Christ, my God, who alone have power to absolve men from their sins, forgive all my transgressions both deliberate and indeliberate, committed in word and in deed. O Lover of mankind, allow me to partake of your divine, glorious and pure mysteries. Let my sharing in your Body and Blood be for the cleansing of my sins and the healing of my body and a pledge of the life to come and of your kingdom. You are the God of mercy! You are loving and kind and full of compassion" (395).

What appears to be a "burning fire consuming the unworthy" is in fact a "gentle dew" of divine grace that cleanses and heals body and soul. "Thou hast vouchsafed, O Lord, that this corruptible temple my human flesh should be united to thy holy flesh, that my blood should be mingled with thine. Therefore, I am thy transparent and translucent member! I am transported out of myself. I am transfigured!" (Symeon the New Theologian).

The Christian knows that the Body and Blood of Christ is the humus where he is planted and the sap that will make him grow in holiness and joy. In Christ he finds life in its highest degree of intensity. His sins are forgiven all his sins and iniquities dissolve in the contact with Christ. The feast of encounter, the supper of love, the vision of the beauty of existence, all find their eternal value in this bodily embrace of Christ. Here is the ferment of immortality and the power of Resurrection. By uniting to our human nature, Christ makes our flesh a part of his divine person. The divine energies penetrate to the very essence of our being and transfigure us into the light of the divinity. Theodore of Cyre wrote: "By eating the Flesh of the Bridegroom and drinking his Blood we enter into the chamber of the nuptial unity."

In receiving the Divine, the Christian becomes a flame of divinity. In accepting the "Gift," he reflects the radiance of divine glory. Here he finds his real self, the dignity and grandeur of his humanity, which is shot through and through and divinity. No wonder that Chrysostom declared the truth of a Christian teaching which we have obscured and forgotten, that "the Christian who ahs attended the Consecration and does not receive the Gifts excommunicates himself from the Church and from God."

Having become one flesh, one soul, and one heart with Christ, the communicant bursts into a hymn of glory and joy, the joy and glory of being and of existing. His feet are indeed on the ground, but his chin is uplifted and his head stretches to the highest heaven. All his senses are awake and vibrant to the presence of Christ:

O You, Who graciously give your flesh to me as food, consuming the
unworthy, consume met not, O my Creator, but rather pass through all the
parts of my body, into all my joints, my heart, my soul. Ever shelter, and
keep me in your love. Chasten me, purify me and control all my passions.
Adorn me. Teach me and enlighten me always. Show me how to be a tab-
ernacle of your Holy Spirit and in no wise the dwelling place of sin. O my
Christ and my God, make me, your child, to be a child of light: for you
alone are the sanctification and the splendor of my whole being (398).

The Christian ascends the Mount of Transfiguration. The
Transfiguration of the Lord on Mount Thabor did not create a new
Christ who did not exist before. Christ was as divine before the
Transfiguration and after it as he was when he made himself visible to
the naked eye of his Apostles: Divinity transcends all human powers
and capabilities and even understanding. To see It, one has to have special eyes, the inner eyes, the eyes of angels, the eyes of God, a divine
grace that alone can open our consciousness and reveal the invisible.
God alone can open such eyes as he opened them for the Apostles at
prayer on the mount.

Three of the four Evangelists, namely, Matthew, Mark and Luke,
describe in their Gospels such a heavenly vision. They grope for words,
but they try to convey what Divinity would look like if we were to see
it like the Apostles did. The flesh which harbors God is full of dazzling
beauty. From this beauty emanates a power which transforms into the
same heavenly beauty even the inanimate matter that touches it, like the
clothes: "His face became resplendent, and as bright as the sun…His
clothes became as white as light…so white and so radiant that no laun-
derer on earth can whiten them in this fashion…" (Matt. 17). The
Christian veneration of the relics of the saints stems from this fact of
the divine penetration of the human body, and through it to clothes, etc.

At the sight of this transformation the "heavens open." The whole
world of God past, present and to come becomes also visible. The past
is symbolized by Moses. The present is in Christ. The future is represented by Elias who is to come again. So Moses and Elias, symbols of
past and future of mankind, are present at the Transfiguration, convers-
ing with Christ who is the now of all times.

The Father on high, seeing that his plan of redemption has been
accomplished, also becomes physically present in the sound of a voice
declaring his delight and pleasure:

'This is my beloved Son…' He who sees such a vision is enraptured and shaken. The Apostles were. Yet they wished it to endure forever. 'How good it is to be here. Let's build a permanent dwelling place and to stay here,' said Peter to the Lord.

Saints as well as many Christian experiencing this same ecstasy wish it to endure for ever and ever :

O Lord and Lover of Mankind, who died and are risen for me, who gave me these life giving gifts for the goof of my body and the sanctification of my soul, make them serve for the healing of my soul and body. Enlighten the eyes of my heart give peace to the powers of my mind. Inspire me with a faith in which there is no shame, a sincere love, a deep wisdom and obedience to your commandments. May they increase in me your divine grace, and make me dwell in your Kingdom. Thus having spent my earthly life, I will one day reach eternal rest where the sound of rejoicing never ceases, where the delight of those who look upon the beauty of your face has no bounds. You are truly the object of our desire and the inexpressible joy of those who love you, Christ our God.

This is the reality of the Christian when he receives Holy Communion. The Christian beholds it and always loves it! It is very sacred, and he treats it as such:

O wonderful,
wonderful
and most wonderful wonderful!
And yet again wonderful (Shakespeare).

Guilt and the sense of guilt does not exist in the Christian. What really does exist in him is awe, admiration and glorification. The Christian is the priest of thanksgiving. "Let our mouth be filled with your praise, O Lord, for you have counted us worthy to share your holy, immortal and spotless mysteries; keep us in sanctification that we may sing your glory, meditating on your holiness all the day long. Alleluia! Alleluia! Alleluia!" This cry of joy and triumph is the echo of what the French wisdom expressed in this saying: "What cannot be spoken must be sung, and what cannot be sung must be danced."

The need to feel space and time is always there in our life, but we can now transcend both space and time and accept the material creation and man and be creative with them. Furthermore, because we have encountered Christ, we can meet with all confidence "the other." For us who receive Communion, every human face is the radiance of the face of Christ. The "other" becomes the sacrament of Christ. Christ in the Bread and the Wine is the ultimate realization of the unity of our human nature both with Christ and with all members of the human race. The "other," therefore, is not a foreigner or a stranger. He is the object and subject of universal communion.

This is life in the Holy Trinity, a "Perichoreisis," a dance, a playful twirl, an "allegro con grazia" which whirls with the elegance of a waltz. Once the Christian has received Christ and realized the real meaning of his life, he is filled with emotion and motion and power. Even when he feels in himself a whole atmosphere of tears he is, underneath it all, a smile. He has discovered the rhythm and movement about and within himself. He might be going through uncertainty, but he always emerges in a dazzling march towards the Light who is Christ. In Holy Communion he reaches an enthralling verve and a breathtaking, dynamic climax. These are really the heroic affirmations of the life-force which is in Christ and which from Christ flows into him. The finale for him is always the eyes of the Gospel illumined with all the glory and beauty of God who is a never ending feast and a supreme celebration.

EPILOGUE

Has Christ succeeded or failed in making the Christian? This question seems to be eating at the hearts of many. Success or failure is generally evaluated according to its immediate and impressive results, according to some sensational impact on one's social surrounding, or by measuring the achievement of something attempted.

After two thousand years of the proclamation of the Gospel, of the preaching of good will and of unlimited and unconditional love, modern civilizations seem to have remained what they were before Christ came. Mammon is still reigning supreme. Fears are on the rise, shattering peaceful relations among men. There is no country where Christ can be said to be a climate, an atmosphere of brotherly relationships, the light and life of the people. Even the Church, as institution, has failed in the creation of such an atmosphere. Was Christ's mission in vain?

In forming Christians, Christ meant to create a "new life." He offered "another life" to transform this life and make it what God meant it to be from the beginning of creation. Christ clothed us with "his life," a life of freedom. He enabled us to live a life of self giving in unlimited and unconditional love. He thus made us sharers in God's life and in his own personal activities and in his own reality, both human and divine.

The "new life" Christ inaugurated is not the end of a process. It is rather a point of departure, the beginning of a long and arduous effort to achieve justice and human fraternity among individuals which will result in fraternity among nations. Above all Christ initiated the consciousness of our divinization, the only road to lasting peace and to the perfect harmony of living with one's self and with the other.

In proposing his teaching about this "new life," Christ proceeds simply and painlessly. His words do not encourage the imagination in its fantasies that things are easy and sweet. The expressions used by the Lord convey the complex problems of life in short metaphors that captivate the heart. Christ talks about the Sower, the Tares, the Weeds of wickedness that grow among the good wheat and that require patience and long suffering to uproot. He talks about Leaven and about the Mustard seed.

The mustard seed is, in fact, the smallest and most insignificant of all seeds. But its insignificant appearance in reality possesses a great potential. Once the mustard seed has died it bursts into a majestic tree where the birds of the sky take refuge and find security and the joy of living. Its development and growth are nothing sensational. It starts rather in death. But life continues silently and secretly in its insignificant appearance hardly attracting attention. Stem and blossom and leaves might wither and perish and be scattered to the four winds, but their movement and work are important and bear life in the fruit.

Christ said that this "new life," "the Kingdom of God," is already present in the hearts of men. He planted its seed. The seed has already died in him and the tree is now growing among men; it will grow within them like the mustard seed. The seed of Christ's life is increasing day by day and secretly transforming human events.

Christ himself is the image and prototype of this "new life." For Christ, apparent failures were really triumphs, successes. Out of his tomb came the splendor of life. Out of the darkness of Hades he ascended into heaven and achieved the supreme and definite triumph of "sitting humanity at the right hand of the Father!" Christ went to sleep and he awoke the dead. When he uttered the words of desperation: "God! My God! Why did you abandon me!" he healed the desperation of mankind and opened to thieves and criminals the gates of "paradise.'

How reassuring is the lesson of Christ's life: success from apparent failure.

Pascal was right when he wrote that "Christ is in agony until the end of the world." Christ will be in agony in Christians because Christians know that the world can never become the place God intended it to be unless they constantly change it and improve it, like water, sun and good soil changes the little seed into a majestic tree. The exquisite joy of great music will never reach us unless we are prepared to study it, to dedicate ourselves to it, and listen to it. Millions of Christians have listened to the Voice, dedicated themselves heroically to its imperatives, and lived the "new life" of the Gospel.

Societies and peoples will listen too. They are already set on fire. Christ's presence in his Body and Blood mingles with the body and blood of mankind, and has been enkindling a flame that will penetrate everything in this world. The atmosphere of peace, of justice, of unlimited and unconditional love is already spreading to the confines of the earth. The spirit of Jesus is flowing like an immense ocean, spreading and inundating the subconscious of men everywhere.

For millions of years, the roots of hatred, division and cruelty have been allowed to grow. If we believe our modern scientists, man has been on earth for several millions of years. Ignorance of himself and of his surroundings created in him fears so deep that his subconscious became infected with terror of himself and of everything he came in contact with. Terror, suspicion, insecurity and therefore hatred became, in fact, his subconscious.

His adventures of all living creatures we can still observe today. Little squirrels, as well as baby lions, meet their new surroundings with bursts of bravado followed by disastrous flight. Their first steps are a blend of caution and boldness, of terror and bliss. For every three steps forward there are two steps backward, mingled with fear.

Instinct has no memory. Once developed, it becomes a sure and fairly accurate means of self preservation in animals. Man has a memory. He stores deep in himself every experience of life. He decodes, edits or discards the messages of life. He analyzes them, mostly to fit his small, subjective games played in darkness and loneliness. Throughout millions of years his intelligence and his five senses were at work, sifting and storing errors and fears. Even the little joys and triumphs were shadowed by the insecurity of ignorance.

Thus man created deep in himself a subconscious, entangled and obscured with suspicion and mistrust, which made him inherently egotistic. Mistrust breeds hatred, and hatred bursts into cruelties more powerful in man than all the blind powers of nature. Mistrust and egotism made man oblivious even to the voice of his maker, God. Is this subconscious what we Christians call "original sin"? Christ came to heal original sin, and restore man to the knowledge of his real self, and to the awareness of his divine origin and destiny as a child of God and united with all living things.

As the rooting of this fearful subconscious was allowed to develop and grow, so its uprooting should be allowed time also. The rooting of Christ's "new life" will soak man's mind and heart and will re create the consciousness of what he really is, divine.

After only two thousand years of Gospel preaching and heroic Christian efforts to grow in the "new life" of Christ, we can observe that ignorance is on the wane and that human hearts are becoming ready to accept the "unacceptable elements" of the Gospel. We see men, the world over, ready to fight against corruption. The flame of the Gospel flickers everywhere, unnoticeably sometimes, but surely and continually. Christ has enkindled a fire, and he does not cease fanning it by his presence until it envelops all humanity. This is the Christian's dream. The Christian dreams with wide open eyes because his eyes are the eyes of the Gospel.

Christ is alive! He has been given as food to the world. He is nourishing creation. The world will grow and flourish into the "new life" of Christ, the life of peace and joy in the celebration of the Feast.

Archbishop Joseph Raya's Publications

Acathist Hymn to the Name of Jesus

Acathist Hymn to the Mother of God

Byzantine Church and Culture

Celebration! Reflections on The Divine and Holy Liturgy

The Divine and Holy Liturgy of Saint John Chrysostom

Christmas: Birth of Our Lord and Saviour Jesus Christ

Metalipsi: Service of Holy Communion without Divine Liturgy

Paraclisis

Theophany and Sacraments of Initiation

Theotokos: Mother of Our Lord and Saviour Jesus Christ

Transfiguration of Our Lord and Saviour Jesus Christ

Archbishop Raya's books can be ordered from
Madonna House Publications
2888 Dafoe Rd
Combermere, Ontario, Canada
K0J 1L0
http://www.madonnahouse.org/publications/raya
1-888-703-7110